HANDBOOK OF STRATEGIC PLANNING FOR NONPROFIT ORGANIZATIONS

HANDBOOK OF STRATEGIC PLANNING FOR NONPROFIT ORGANIZATIONS

Siri N. Espy

PRAEGER

New York
Westport, Connecticut
London

Copyright Acknowledgment
A quotation from Lewis Carroll, *Alice in Wonderland*, edited
by Donald J. Gray (W. W. Norton & Co., Inc., 1971), has
been reprinted with permission.

Library of Congress Cataloging-in-Publication Data
Espy, Siri N.
   Handbook of strategic planning for nonprofit organiza-
tions.

   Bibliography: p.
   Includes index.
   1. Corporations, Nonprofit—Planning.
2. Corporations, Nonprofit—Management.   3. Strategic
planning.   I. Title.
HD62.6.E86   1986   658.1'148   86-21192
ISBN 0-275-92342-8 (alk. paper)

Library of Congress Catalog Card Number: 86-21192
ISBN: 0–275–92342–8

First published in 1986

Praeger Publishers, One Madison Avenue, New York, NY 10010
An imprint of Greenwood Publishing Group, Inc.

Printed in the United States of America

The paper used in this book complies with the Permanent
Paper Standard issued by the National Information Standards
Organization (Z39.48–1984).

10 9 8 7 6 5 4

This book is dedicated to the discovery
that growth can come from frustration
and order from chaos

Contents

 # Acknowledgments

In any undertaking of this magnitude, there are a number of influences that encourage the writer to be a writer. In this regard, I must thank the staff of Gateway Rehabilitation Center, which gave me the opportunity to learn and provided the environment in which such a project is possible.

I am grateful to my family for their support and belief in me, and to William for understanding, putting up with me, and helping me to get up in the morning.

HANDBOOK OF STRATEGIC PLANNING FOR NONPROFIT ORGANIZATIONS

1

Why Strategic Planning?

"Would you tell me, please, which way I ought to go from here?"
"That depends a good deal on where you want to get to," said the Cat.
"I don't much care where," said Alice.
"Then it doesn't matter which way you go," said the Cat.
"So long as I get *somewhere*," Alice added as an explanation.
"Oh, you're sure to do that," said the Cat, "if you only walk long enough."

Lewis Carroll, *Alice in Wonderland*

Your organization is going somewhere. This can be construed as a statement of optimism, but it is also a statement of fact. Within the next five years, your organization will have changed in some way; even a decision not to change will not halt the progress of the external environment and your organization's position in it. Your awareness of this obvious but somewhat uncomfortable reality can mean the difference between success and failure for your organization.

Strategic planning has been highly touted and made to sound like an almost mystical process from which an organizational direction will magically emerge. In reality, strategic planning is a simple acknowledgment that your organization is in fact going somewhere, and a means of creating a favorable future.

Most organizations are experienced in formulating annual goals and objectives, developing a budget, and scheduling routine activities. Strategic planning shares some fundamental concepts with these activities, but differs in that it addresses the development of an overall direction or strategy for the organization. Ideally, it provides a framework within which these other activities can occur.

The terms "strategic planning" and "long-range planning" are sometimes used interchangeably, but there are important differences between the two. Strategic planning is focused on reaching specific, well-defined goals designed to benefit the organization as a whole. It is certainly possible to have a number of long-range goals and plans that are quite independent of one another and in fact lead in different directions. Strategic planning is a means of making some very fundamental decisions and charting a course so that your short- and long-range planning is more efficiently focused and integrated.

The differences and relationships among strategic, long-range, and short-range planning are important to clearly understand early in the process:

- Strategic planning defines organization-wide goals, directions, or destinations. It defines a strategy for success.
- Long-range planning is the development of plans to address a multi-year time period. An organization's long-range plans will hopefully be geared toward reaching goals outlined in the strategic plan.
- Short-range planning can be thought of as addressing a period of one year or less. Annual goals and objectives are one example; an organization might also develop short-range plans to deal with a specific situation, problem, or crisis. Ideally, short-range plans will move toward implementation of the long-range plan, which in turn will support the strategic plan.

Strategic planning deals with some very fundamental questions of organizational identity and integrity. It assumes a willingness to take an honest look at the entire operation with an eye to improvement and change. Planning can be somewhat threatening to existing structures, but the payoff of taking a serious look at your organization can be well worth the investment.

Successful strategic planning does not filter down from bureaucratic ivory towers. It is a reality-based activity carried out by and in consultation with those who are responsible for the organization's daily operations. Strategic planning has the greatest chance of successful development and implementation when it is an activity involving the staff who will be impacted by the plan. Rather than being the exclusive domain of specialized and sophisticated planners, strategic planning is an opportunity for staff at all levels to have a voice in the future of the organization.

The development of a strategic plan is more an art than a science; while there are techniques and guidelines available, the process depends largely on the abilities and thinking of the persons involved. The identification and development of corporate values, which are central to the planning process, can only be achieved through imagination, vision, and creativity. Giving planning serious thought and consideration is a tough but very real responsibility.

Organizational planning and management can be rather simply broken down into three levels: strategic, tactical, and operational:

The strategic level involves mapping out the overall course that the organization will follow. It is aimed at developing concepts and ideas that will guide the organization over a period of time. The strategy is the destination and overall direction of the organization. Planning at the strategic level is generally thought of as the function of top management.

The tactical level is the development of specific means for achieving the strategy. It is the formulation of specific, concrete goals and objectives to help the organization reach its chosen destination. Planning at this level is analogous to determining which highways will provide the most direct and easily traveled route to the destination. Tactical planning might be carried out by top and middle managers in a larger organization where several levels of management exist.

The operational level is the day-to-day, nuts and bolts execution of strategy and tactics. It is the switch-on of the ignition and progress toward a specified destination. Planning at this level is often thought of as the responsibility of lower-level managers within a more complex organizational structure.

Clearly, all three levels are vital to good management. Without the destination, roadmap, and reliable transportation, your chances of a good trip are greatly reduced. Strategic planning is a means whereby your staff can closely examine your options and attempt to develop a concrete, workable map to follow. Unlike annual goals and objectives, strategic planning addresses a multi-year period and extends into your organization's future, recognizing that realistically, not all of your goals can be developed and achieved in a one-year period. The strategic plan, then, will be the guiding force behind the development of annual goals and objectives for the next several years.

Strategic planning tends to be market oriented. Clearly, it is in your best interest to offer services for which there is a market or audience. A vital part of strategic planning as opposed to other types of planning is the development of a marketing strategy. In order to do what you do well and effectively, your organization must be known and accessible. As part of the planning process, marketing issues will be explored. You will identify your constituency and "stakeholders"—those who are affected by your actions and invested in your survival.

The strategic planning process will take you from hopes and dreams for your organization's future to the actual possibilities and situations you must face. It begins with looking at possibilities, daydreaming, brainstorming, and "blue sky" thinking, and progresses to the gritty realities of the world around you. It forces a careful and thoughtful look at the givens, the options, and the *shoulds*. It can help to move your organization forward in the best possible direction.

WHY BOTHER TO PLAN?

Many nonprofits feel a basic reluctance to enter into the strategic planning process for a number of reasons:

We Don't Know Where to Begin or How to Plan

It is true that most nonprofit agencies do not employ MBAs sophisticated in planning and business management. However, your organization undoubtedly has a valuable asset: expertise in what you do. A thorough understanding of your field should not be underestimated as a resource. You are very likely familiar with your service area, other agencies doing similar work, and trends in the field. This expertise will prove invaluable in the planning process. There are resources available (such as this book) to help you with the technicalities. But don't be intimidated by the complexity of the process; the skills and resources are probably right at your fingertips.

Nonprofit Organizations Really Don't Need Strategic Planning

Like it or not, a nonprofit is a business that bears fundamental similarities to any other business. You have a staff, a budget, resources to allocate, funding sources, and expenditures. There are decisions to be made in all these areas that will greatly impact on the future of your organization. A worthy goal is to become a profitable nonprofit so you will have the flexibility to better serve your constituency. In order to do this effectively, you will need to develop a "business plan" that will help you to make the decisions that face you on a daily basis.

While revenue from nonprofit organizations does not provide direct financial benefit to individuals, their services and undertakings do affect the lives of many. Good strategic management can be beneficial even if your only goal is to continue serving the needs of your target population in a similar manner. Just keeping up with reality can be quite a challenge.

We Don't Have the Time for All This

Putting out fires is unfortunately and frequently the primary activity of managers everywhere. Legitimate crises can chase you relentlessly, and the demands of day-to-day operations can be exhausting. Everything needs to be done, and work piles up. It is always difficult to set aside time for a process that will not immediately bear fruit; it is easy to put off until tomorrow when today's demands are so persistent. But don't forget that your organization is going somewhere; day by day, without your knowledge or permission, the world is changing and your organization is reaching decision points. If ignored, these decisions are made in a haphazard way that may lead your organization in an unfavorable direction. The only way to take control of this process is to make decisions in a systematic way that leads to a planned and desired result.

Our Staff Is Too Small

If your staff is large enough to work, it is large enough to plan. Granted, a small staff may not need or be able to produce a sophisticated plan. But every staff can spend some time looking at options and directions and making some fundamental decisions, most of which will be made anyway by omission or trial and error. With fewer hands, the work may be heavier and specific expertise lacking. However, you can still adopt a strategic framework for your decisions and management.

We Just Survive from Day to Day

Wouldn't you like to be able to stop living only from day to day? While planning is certainly no panacea, it can help provide some security by building a framework for decisions and actions. The development of a well thought-out plan can also help you to tackle the problems that interfere with the organization's ability to project its activities and strategies into the future. It can help you to deal with issues like funding, development, marketing, and new services that might put your organization in a position to live on a basis that is more secure than day to day, hand to mouth.

Our Basic Mission Is Mandated by An Outside Body, So We Don't Need to Plan

Even if your services are well defined by an outside group, you still probably make choices on how, when, where, or to whom the services will be provided. In this position, there may be more givens to accept, and your goal may be to provide your services in a more cost-effective or efficient way, to reach additional clients, or to find more creative ways of operating. Nearly every organization has some autonomy, and that autonomy can be the basis of a plan for being even better at what you do.

Things Change So Fast, There's No Point to Planning

The point to planning is that things do change very rapidly. A plan is never cast in concrete, and needs to be flexible in order to accommodate reality. Contingencies need to be very carefully considered, and the plan will need periodic revisions. The planning process, however, is a means of monitoring the external environment and developing strategies for dealing with change. Attempting to stand still during change is rarely successful; the evolution of external realities will inevitably alter the position of your organization in the environment.

SO WHERE DOES THIS LEAVE US?

Why should you plan? There are a number of very good reasons for taking a hard look at your organization.

Creating a Future

The idea of creating a future may sound very lofty, and we all know that reality is waiting for us at every turn. But to the extent possible, it is the administrator's obligation to take the organization in a favorable direction. And how do you know what is favorable until you identify your options and analyze the pros and cons of each? It is impossible to create (or even influence) the future without an active effort on your part. It is possible to plan for a future that will be favorable and beneficial to you.

Planning for Allocation of Resources

Planning for resource allocation is especially important to nonprofit agencies with limited resources. How do you know how to spend your dollars without clear priorities and goals? The development of a workable plan can help your organization to spend wisely and divide the pie in a way that moves you a step closer to your ultimate goals. Budgeting and resource allocation must be done in any case. Why not do it in a thoughtful manner?

Fund Raising

Development is a necessary but complicated and difficult aspect of nonprofit management. As competition increases for donations, each organization will be in a position of having to justify and court every dollar won. The development of a sound strategic plan can help you to present your organization clearly and convincingly to potential donors. With a clear knowledge of where the money is going and why, donors may be more impressed with your organization and its mission. A good plan is also needed to carry out fund-raising activities, and this may be a focus of the planning process. Strategic planning can help you to identify and package your needs in a way that will be attractive to potential donors, and will help you to be sure that your needs are funded in the best way possible.

Competition

This formerly dirty word is indeed a factor in nonprofit management. Although in a larger sense we may all be operating for the greater good, it is important to be aware of who is competing with you for clients, funding, space, or other resources. As a manager, you will need to develop strategies for making certain your organization gets its fair share (at least!) of the goods. Planning is greatly influenced by the competitive picture and the actions of others around you. Whether you ultimately decide to compete or work cooperatively with other agencies, or combine the two, it is essential to know who is out there, what they are doing, and how they might affect you.

Coordination of Efforts

In a larger agency composed of several departments or divisions, or even within a single department, different ideas, strategies, and tactics can emerge. It will not benefit your organization to be a house divided. By pulling together on the development of an organizational strategy, all parties can begin to see the big picture and their role in carrying the organization closer to identified goals. This overall strategy can provide a framework for decisions and actions in all departments and on all levels.

Team Building

Any observer of a tug of war can attest to the importance of teammates all pulling in the same direction. The management of an organization is very much the same. Planning gives all the members of your team a chance to be heard and to work together toward common goals. This can prove to be an invigorating and exciting experience (with a few inevitable detours), and can help your staff to achieve a sense of common purpose.

Just Plain Good Management

Without a clear map, it is difficult to tell exactly where to go. While some managers may be blessed with impeccable instincts, the rest of us need to think, plan, and organize our work. It is difficult to be a top-notch manager or administrator without an idea of where you are going. And the best way of knowing where you are going is to plan!

CAUTION!

Now that you are aware of the virtues of planning, several cautions are in order. While there are some very good reasons to plan, there are some equally good reasons not to. They include the following:

We Really Just Need to Get Something Down on Paper

Strategic planning as a paper exercise is bad form. There is nothing more frustrating than expending time and energy on a project that has no chance of being taken seriously. Even to look good on paper, a plan requires some commitment of resources. If you are required or requested to develop a plan, why not put in enough energy to make the plan meaningful and useful? The staff will be justified in its bad morale if the organizational plan becomes a shelf ornament following their investment in its creation.

We Lack Commitment from the Top

While this obstacle may be overcome by persuasion, politicking and maneuvering, it can be fatal. The planning process needs the commitment and leadership of top management and the board of directors. While there are ways to sell others on the importance of organizational planning, it is important to be certain they are sold. Passivity or obstructionism can be deadly diseases to the planning process and the extent to which the final product is taken seriously.

We Really Don't Intend to Change

If this statement is true of your organization, then the undertaking of a planning process may be a futile task. The prognosis for your organization is also probably poor. A good idea might be to run a diagnostic check on the agency to attempt to define the illness that is creating this attitude. Is it burnout? Lack of challenge? Poor leadership? It's important for any business, profit or nonprofit, to be open to change and ready to seize opportunities. Try to engender some enthusiasm and enrich the lifeblood of your organization. The planning process may help to create some enthusiasm and creativity if a spark of energy can be lighted.

HOW THIS BOOK CAN HELP

Unfortunately, there are no magic formulas for success. The material contained in this book is intended to provide you with some guidelines, ideas, and structures for both strategic and long-range planning that may fit your organization. Adapting and choosing selectively what you think will work for you is the best use of this information. If you make every attempt to tailor the process to your own needs, the plan is likely to be more meaningful.

The scope and complexity of the process can and should be tailored to suit the needs of the organization. Small staffs will realistically need to modify some of this material to fit limited personpower and resources. Obviously, multiple planning committees cannot exist with a total staff of three, but the basic structure can be adapted to a staff of any size.

Even if you decide that now is not the time to undertake the development of an actual plan, some of the suggestions offered here may help you to manage strategically or provide a framework for projects that you plan to carry out. Any decision you make can be better made in terms of your organization's overall goals and directions. Developing some statements of organizational strategy can be a boon to the administrator in controlling and evaluating progress.

If you've ever tried to explain, step by step, how to tie a shoe, you know that the explanation is very difficult and makes the process of shoe-tying sound awfully complex. The explanation of planning can likewise sound more difficult than the process itself. Overcoming inertia and getting rolling might be the most difficult part. A nicely tied shoe can be the reward.

Roadblocks always arise, and the planning process is like any other managerial task in that solving a problem is likely to create two more. With some courage, foresight, and sheer determination, however, any nonprofit organization can forge ahead with a plan and come out the better for it.

2

_____ Planning to Plan

> The measure of success is not whether you have a tough
> problem to deal with, but whether it's the same problem you had
> last year.
>
> John Foster Dulles

Like any other project or management function, the planning process itself requires careful planning. Abruptly calling your management team or staff together and announcing, "Today we will do a strategic plan," would meet with confusion, dismay, and dead air. It's important to do your homework and map out what you want to accomplish. This alone is an important and difficult task.

In order to begin the planning process effectively and efficiently, a number of fundamental questions need to be answered, and several areas must be addressed.

WHY ARE WE DOING THIS?

Chances are that your organization has survived for a number of years without a formal strategic plan. So why now? It is important to clarify your reasons for undertaking this venture at this point in time. As we discussed in the last chapter, there are a number of very good reasons to plan. Identifying your primary motivation will help you to tailor the planning process to your needs and is the first step toward achieving favorable results. Making a list of your needs and expectations for the planning process is an excellent place to start. The list might include items like this:

- We need additional sources of revenue and aren't sure how to proceed.
- There is a need in our community for more youth programming and we don't know if or how we can fill it.
- Our community hospital is losing patients to one of our competitors and we need a strategy to fight back.
- We need to undertake a fund-raising campaign and aren't sure how to identify and package our needs.
- There is a large herd of sacred cows grazing on our lawn which is impeding our growth and progress.

Your list may resemble the above, and will probably include several items. Look at it, discuss it with others on the staff and board of directors, and expand it if possible. Then, go back over it and prioritize. Look at what you believe will be your most urgent needs over the next several years. Identify possibilities and stated goals for the organization. Try to begin defining the most important areas for the agency's growth and development. By identifying your top priorities, you have taken an important step toward developing an effective strategic plan. This is where your expertise at what you do becomes essential and invaluable. Your knowledge of your organization's needs will help you to tailor the plan to those needs and help you to solve identified problems.

As you develop your "plan for planning," keep in mind all areas you hope to address and develop plans for. You might want to take a close look at your existing services, develop new ones, or concentrate on an area such as fund raising or corporate structure. It is very likely that new ideas and directions will develop serendipitously from the process, but careful exploration will allow you to be certain to address your unique needs.

WHO'S RUNNING THE SHOW?

As in any other task, clear lines of authority and responsibility need to be outlined for the planning process. The director or chief executive officer will certainly play a pivotal role, and may in many organizations be the logical person to be "in charge" of the planning process. However, there are also times when it is logical and beneficial to delegate this task to another member of the staff. This would be especially appropriate if there is a staff member who has more time, interest, or inclination toward planning. If the leadership of the strategic planning process is delegated, there are a number of factors to consider:

- The leader should have a good knowledge of the workings of the organization and be able to see the "big picture."
- Full support of the top administrator is essential and must be clearly stated from the outset.

- The designate should be well organized, compulsive, and able to get things done and motivate others.
- There should be some consideration of the other duties of the position, and some temporary help provided if necessary and feasible.
- Preferably, the "planner" should be relatively free of turf issues or at least be able to look at situations objectively.

It is vitally important that someone "own" primary responsibility for getting the plan done. While planning is a team effort, many staff members may be tempted to retreat into the safer and more pressing business of putting out fires. It's necessary to keep on plugging and continually push the process along. Ultimately, the chief executive officer will need to make sure the project is running smoothly and is being taken seriously; lending clout to the process at its earliest stages will help to legitimize it and emphasize its priority status.

The person who is in charge of the planning process should be designated as chairperson of the planning committee. It is important that duties and responsibilities be clearly outlined; for example:

The chairperson will coordinate and oversee all aspects of the planning process and serve on all project teams; will call and chair all planning committee meetings; will monitor the progress of all project teams, and approve any changes in the directions of the planning process in consultation with the planning committee; will coordinate all information released concerning the planning process and work with staff and board of directors as necessary; will be responsible for producing the final planning document, subject to review and approval by the planning committee.

By clearly defining roles, there is less room for confusion and buckpassing. Especially if the planning responsibility is delegated, it is essential that both the planner and fellow employees understand the authority, responsibilities, and duties of the position.

DOING YOUR HOMEWORK

Once the designation of primary responsibility has been made, the information-gathering process can begin in earnest. Commit yourself to learning as much as you can about the *hows* and *whys* of strategic planning. Read about planning in books, journals, and periodicals. Note facts or concepts that may be relevant or useful to your planning process. Attend some seminars or training sessions if you can locate and afford them. Talk with others who have successfully completed a strategic plan. The exchange of ideas can be a valuable resource; while you may not want to share information freely with your competitors, there may be different types of organizations from which you can learn. Even corporate planners in for-profit businesses might prove to be valuable sources of information. While realistically you may not become a leading expert in the field of organizational planning, you can discover a great deal about planning by nosing around and being willing to learn.

LOOKING FOR INFORMATION

The development of a successful plan depends on accurate, timely information on which to base your judgment and conclusions. Very early in the process, it pays to begin identifying what types of information you will need. Pertinent data can be divided into two types, internal and external.

Internal data is related to the program itself; it is relevant to the analysis of available facts about your organization and its operations. Internal data might include:

• The number of persons served by the organization on an annual basis
• Revenue and expense figures for the past five years
• A breakdown of the population served by your organization by age, sex, marital status, and income
• The qualifications and background of your staff

Internal data can help you to learn more about your organization and provide input for objective assessments in important areas.

External data is related to the environment in which your organization operates. It can include:

• The median income of households in nearby areas
• An annual report of one of your competitors
• Articles or other information on trends in your field
• Population demographics and projections in your service area
• Estimates of the prevalence of problems with which your agency is concerned
• Studies on the effectiveness of various treatments or programs

External data will help you to understand the climate of the world around you, and will assist you in making decisions on the directions your organization might take.

Both internal and external data can be used to examine the past and present, and to project into the future. By looking at data over time, trends can be detected. One-quarter of financial losses by a program can be a fluke or the result of one bad decision; two years of steady losses paints an entirely different picture, which will affect the future of that program. Examining data on past performance can also help you to understand how you have arrived at your present position, and can assist in planning for future growth.

By looking at relevant data over time, it is possible to learn a great deal about your organization and its environment. Making some wise and selective decisions regarding your information needs will help you to be enlightened without entering the realm of "infomania." Irrelevant or overabundant data can easily cause as much confusion as too little. Try to pinpoint your unique information needs, identify potential sources, and begin doing some digging.

Remember that data is only as good as its consumers. What does it mean that 12 percent of your clients come from the next county? Who cares that 42 percent of the children enrolled in your program are boys? This information alone reveals little; the art of management and planning is the ability to interpret data and turn it into useful information. By examining data within the framework of your needs, operating history, and goals for the future, it can prove immensely valuable.

Now is the time to begin looking for and collecting both internal and external data. Whether your management information system consists of sophisticated hardware and software or a crew of volunteers compiling information from your files, it is important to centralize data collection. Start sending interesting articles, brochures, and materials from your competitors and internal reports to a central person or place. Scattered bits and pieces are of little value in looking at the big picture.

BASIC STRATEGY

It's time to begin to think about your organization's basic strategy: where you want to go, what you want to be. Think, and ask other good thinkers and key staff (hopefully one and the same) to do so also. You may already have a fairly clear idea of where you want to arrive within the next few years. Try to begin articulating your goals and thinking of possible time frames for the achievement of those items. Maybe you can already state:

- We want to capture at least half of the home health care market in our service area within the next two years.
- Increasing our services to teenage mothers by a factor of two within five years is our major objective.
- We plan to be the leading provider of services to disabled children in our county.
- Our goal is to add a publishing business for educational materials to our existing services.
- Finding new sources of revenue must be our primary goal over the next three years.

If you can begin to articulate these basic, fundamental goals for your organization, this will help to unify and focus your plan. Identifying your primary goals will help to plan your efforts and will make the next step even easier. Also, at this point you should begin to define the time period over which the plan should extend. Be realistic. Strategic planning has been defined in five- or ten-year increments, which may not be feasible for your organization, depending on the trends and changes in your field.

At this stage, conclusions reached will almost certainly be preliminary; it is the function of strategic planning to determine whether these preliminary notions are in fact feasible or desirable for your organization. Like any hypothesis, preliminary thoughts on organizational strategy are testable educated guesses. Through the planning process, you will be gathering data and using the collective wisdom of your staff to determine whether these directions will in fact be the most beneficial for your organization.

Examination of existing program documents can be a good place to start in thinking about organizational strategy issues. Examine the goals and objectives, meeting minutes, budgets and financial statements, and the records of staff activities. What areas have been priorities in the past? What programs have been identified as particularly beneficial or of questionable value to the organization? What roadblocks have been experienced and what opportunities have existed over the past several years? By reflecting on these questions and examining the history of your organization, you can uncover some valuable clues to the areas that warrant consideration as elements of the strategic plan.

Being open to change will allow you to consider yet other possibilities as your work on the plan progresses. You may find that your original instincts and educated guesses were right on target, but if they pose insurmountable problems, you may find yourself in search of new ideas or workable variants of the old ones. Developing a preliminary idea of possible strategies will provide a starting point, but may be subject to change as the facts and alternatives come into focus.

THE PLAN FOR PLANNING

When a lucky soul is designated as "chief planner," the first task to be undertaken is the development of a plan for planning. This need not be elaborate, but should clearly state why the plan is being undertaken and what you hope to accomplish. It should include major areas to be addressed, assignment of responsibility, and the formation of planning groups or project teams. This plan should be complete, clear, and specific, so that when it has been carried out your primary goals to be addressed in the planning process have been met.

The development of a clear "plan for planning" outlines your goals and mission in the planning process. It should minimize wheel-spinning and foster commonness of purpose. This plan should be reviewed, discussed, and dissected. If successful, it will outline the major contents of your eventual organizational plan. Careful scrutiny at this point will minimize omissions and useless work as you proceed.

Your plan for planning will need to allow for examination of some fundamental issues, such as your mission, philosophy, and corporate structure, unless you are very sure that these are entirely satisfactory and will carry you on to a better future. Remember, planning requires a clear and thorough examination of your organization from the top down.

Sketching out your structure, in the form of an organizational chart, may help you to see how to best achieve your purposes. This is another step toward covering all your bases and clearly outlining authority and accountability. The structure might include elements such as appear in Figure 2.1. By fleshing out the structure, you begin dividing your issues into logical areas so that they can be tackled in the most efficient way. Issues tend to overlap and interrelate, and work on related issues can be coordinated. Experimenting with this model can help you to determine the best way to deal with the issues you have identified as important for your organization.

THE PLANNING COMMITTEE

In most cases, you will find it helpful to put together a designated planning committee that will hold primary responsibility for overseeing the process, discussing the direction it is taking, and making final decisions on plans and priorities. This group must include the top administrator, and should in most cases include all top-level staff. These are the individuals who will hold ultimate responsibility for the organization, and therefore its plans, and it is important that they have a role in its development. Also, by their input and expertise you maximize your chances of developing a plan that will best serve your organization and has the best chance of actually being followed once completed. This group will serve as an executive committee to whom all other planning groups or task forces will report.

The planning committee should meet initially to review the planning needs of the organization, set up the structure and deadlines, and try to arrive at common goals. This group should receive minutes of all planning meetings, and assemble periodically to review the work as it progresses. They should also have the ability to authorize or veto new directions that may arise unpredictably during the process. This group will eventually be responsible for reviewing the final reports on each issue and setting the course and direction the plan will take. This is a new major responsibility, and its importance will need to be impressed upon all the participants.

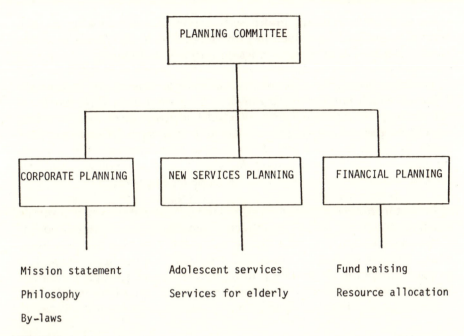

Fig. 2.1
Organizational chart

PROJECT TEAMS

Especially in larger organizations where some specialization or variety of functions may occur, the development of project teams will be an important part of the planning process. A project team is simply a group of staff members brought together for a designated period of time to complete a specific, well-defined task. These groups will serve to carry out the groundwork in a number of areas.

If your organization has identified the development of new services as a priority, a project team can be put together whose function is to explore all aspects of proposed services in depth. The team should be composed of those responsible for or knowledgeable about the issue, along with any other staff members whose knowledge, viewpoints, or creativity may be valuable. The group's task will be to develop a proposal for that service. They may need to do some reading and research on similar projects, check out who else is providing a similar service, look at staffing needs, develop a budget, examine the pros and cons of adding the service, and look at a possible timetable for the project. By dealing clearly with this issue, the project team is focused and has a well-defined task that can be completed. A final report will then be submitted to the planning committee for review and recommendations.

For example, a planning group with responsibility for looking into the feasibility and steps involved in providing a Meals on Wheels program for the elderly might have its mission outlined as follows:

Investigate whether it is feasible and desirable for this agency to develop a Meals on Wheels program for the elderly in this county. Look at the number of elderly within the county and projected population figures for the next five years. Look at the costs and revenues associated with the project. Determine staffing needs, as well as the possibility of recruiting and retaining volunteer help. Do an analysis of the pros and cons of this service. Develop a proposed timetable for implementation of this project should we decide to proceed.

Project teams can also be formed to look critically at the organization's existing structures, and develop recommendations for changes and improvements. A project team can work on the development of a long-range funding strategy, corporate restructuring, or the improvement of present marketing efforts. By putting together small groups, a number of issues can be tackled within the framework of the planning process.

Having a number of project teams can accomplish several things:

- The work is broken down into manageable chunks and does not seem quite so overwhelming.
- The project teams can involve staff most knowledgeable about an issue and exclude others who are not involved with the issue. Realistically, this acknowledges that those who are experts in one area may lack knowledge in another, and allows the organization to best utilize available resources.
- More staff can be involved in planning, which is good for overall morale and creating enthusiasm for the agency.
- The staff is not spread as thin. By dividing the workload, it puts less of a burden on individual members of the staff.

There is one danger in project teams that can be overcome by (again) careful planning: chaos and lack of coordination. It is possible to create a whole system of satellites spinning in their own independent orbits and taking on a life of their own. It is also possible for several groups to duplicate the work of their cohorts. Ideally, the overall coordinator of the planning process can be a member of each group, so that one person can be involved in all aspects of the planning. If that is not feasible, then the "planner" should carefully monitor minutes for signs of trouble. Periodic reviews of all groups' work by the planning committee will also be helpful in ensuring coordination and commonness of purpose.

Each project team will need a designated chairperson whose duties will include calling and running meetings, assigning tasks, seeing that minutes are taken, and writing reports. Again, careful selection is important. If at all possible, the person who is responsible for the area under consideration should be put in charge of the project. This person should have expertise in the area, and you may be treading on a political minefield to bypass a responsible person for leadership of the project team. Project team chairpersons need clear direction, encouragement, assistance, and a shoulder to cry on at times. Be sure to provide all of the above!

WHO TO INVOLVE

Deciding on who to involve is indeed a difficult issue to settle. There are staff members who want no part of planning, those who would like to be involved, and those who will be mortally wounded if they are not involved every step of the way. There are very talented people at lower levels and not-so-talented people close to the top. There are excellent thinkers who function very poorly in groups and others who talk better than they think. So how do you resolve the dilemma of who to involve?

There are those who, by virtue of their position, will probably need to be involved regardless of their weaknesses. For example, it is difficult to imagine developing a useful financial plan without the input of the financial officer, even if he or she is very difficult to work with or resistant to involvement. Heads of departments or functions that are the focus of planning activities must also be involved; a good rule of thumb is to include anyone in developing the plan who will be responsible for implementing it. Otherwise, you are setting up a situation that is likely to result in sabotage or lack of cooperation. By all means, involve good thinkers—bright, creative people who can add a spark or look at things from a different perspective. In fact, this may be a good opportunity to give some credit and additional responsibility to a "rising star" within your organization, and can help to groom such persons for eventual promotion.

Be prepared for a few temper tantrums or hurt feelings from those who are not as involved in the planning process as they had hoped. But do plan to involve your entire staff at some point. "Brainstorming" sessions with them as part of the planning process can be valuable in terms of both input and morale. This way, staff who do not play a major role can be assured that their views and suggestions will be heard and respected.

THE BOARD OF DIRECTORS

Relationships between agency staffs and boards of directors can range from friendly and supportive to hostile and adversarial. However, the board will not go away, and it is important to acknowledge this fact in the planning process. Your board must eventually be involved in your plan, perhaps in authorizing expenditures or approving new services, so it will be to your advantage to get their support and input early in the process. Members of your board may have expertise or access to resources that will be valuable to you, so think about how the board may be beneficial to the planning process.

Planning is also an excellent way to involve the board more in your organization, if that is your goal. This can be an exciting, stimulating, and challenging time in the life of the organization, and can provide an excellent opportunity for board development. Since nonprofit boards tend to be volunteers with busy lives of their own, their investment in and attention to your organization can be minimal. However, everyone appreciates being needed and involved, and this provides a good opportunity. Members of the board of directors can serve on committees or project teams, or can be appointed as advisors to such groups. They can be called on as "experts" in some areas under consideration, and can assist with some of the leg work if they are willing. By generating enthusiasm in your board for the planning process, you may also find heightened enthusiasm for your organization as a whole.

It is not surprising that people who feel that they have helped to give birth to an idea will feel more invested in its success. Board involvement in the plan can ensure their wholehearted backing when the plan is implemented. They will know what you are doing and why, and may be more willing to get involved in fund raising for a program they know and love.

WHAT'S OUR HURRY?

It bears repeating that planning can assume last priority on the busy schedules of your staff. They may be legitimately overworked, resistant to change, reluctant to take on more work, or (God forbid) just plain lazy. The importance of deadlines is paramount in a planning project. Perhaps you already have a deadline in mind, based on your needs or the demands of the world around you. If you plan to begin a fund-raising campaign next June, or a new agency is opening in December that intends to steal your clients, these factors may tend to "mandate" deadlines. But even if it seems as though you have all the time in the world, beware! A project such as this can easily expand to fill "all the time in the world" if it is not carefully planned and monitored. Set a reasonable deadline in light of the goals you are mapping out, staffing, external demands, and other pertinent factors. Set target dates for interim reports or committee recommendations that may be assigned. Set *the* date by which the plan is to be completed. Then be prepared to stick to it, mention it often, and circle it in red on the calendars of the staff.

It's easy to become bogged down and delay or give up on what you are doing. Keep up a brisk pace toward your goal. Let your staff know that the word "dead" is not a part of "deadline" by accident. And mean it.

3

_____ Corporate Identity and Directions

At some point in the life-cycle of virtually every organization,
its ability to succeed in spite of itself runs out.

Richard Brien

Defining the nature and purpose of your organization is a basic task in the planning process, and one that may prove to be more difficult than it sounds. Without clear knowledge of your present whereabouts, it is difficult to progress to setting goals for your organization. As you begin the planning process, a number of identified issues unique to your organization will be explored. However, there are also some fundamental issues that warrant exploration and clarification in any organization. One of the basics, marketing issues, will be explored in Chapter 5, and must be kept in mind when dealing with other planning issues. Other fundamental issues of corporate identity and organizational definition must be addressed early in the planning process.

FUNDAMENTAL ORGANIZATIONAL ISSUES

A first step in determining your destination is to get a firm fix on your present location. Planning a trip to Denver will be a very different task depending on whether you are starting out from Boulder or Bangor. Taking a good look at your present position and corporate identity will provide information that is fundamental to taking the next step. Although you work in the organization and perhaps spend most of your waking hours within its walls, it is easy to glide along without ever examining some of the most basic issues of all.

What Business Are We in?

The immediate answer to a simple question such as this is, "Of course, we are in the business of:

- Providing housing to the homeless, OR
- Offering education to adults, OR
- Sheltering abused women, OR
- Helping families reduce debt and budget resources."

However, on closer examination, these answers are probably oversimplifications and fail to give your organization credit for all the many tasks and ancillary services that are involved in your overall operation. Stop and think about what you actually do. An agency for the homeless might also provide meals, access to clothing, counseling, recreation, information on employment, and referrals to other agencies for medical care. This list differs greatly from the simple statement, "We provide housing to the homeless," and it more fully describes what your organization actually does. It also more clearly accounts for where resources are spent, and may help to pinpoint areas where needs exist.

By taking a close, careful look at what business you are actually in, you can begin both to enumerate and eventually to summarize the various aspects of the service you provide. You may find that your organization is creeping into areas of service that were never formally planned for or approved. You may also find that less time and resources are being allocated for what was once your primary service. These shifts in service delivery are normal and healthy for any organization as long as they are recognized and dealt with in a productive manner. By acknowledging that your business may not be what it was or what you thought it to be, you begin to open the door to a careful exploration of your needs and options.

Shifts in the definition of your business are inevitable and the need for redefinition does not mean that your organization has failed. Trends in the provision of health care toward outpatient services, the move toward deinstitutionalization and mainstreaming, the legalization of abortion, and the shortage of adoptable babies are all examples of forces which over the years have driven many nonprofit organizations to redefine what business they are in. In the day-to-day climate of putting out fires and survival, some of these changes can be assimilated into various parts of the organization without their importance and impact being fully recognized. The exploration and definition of what business you are in will help you to better define and get in touch with the realities around you.

Once you have detailed the nuts and bolts of your organization, your next task is to capture its essence. Summarizing a variety of services is not an easy task, yet it is important to identify the central concept or concepts around which your agency is organized and attempt to define your services accordingly.

Look at the difference between the following two statements:

"We are in the business of providing services to abused children."

"Our organization provides group, individual, and family counseling to abused children and their families. We assist with referrals to public assistance, legal aid, mental health, medical care, and other needed services. We work closely with the local children's services agency to provide for foster care or temporary shelter where needed. We provide volunteers to assist stressed or high-risk parents in coping with their children. Our goal is to support and educate families to eliminate abusive patterns and foster healthy interactions."

Certainly, the second statement gives the reader a much clearer idea of the organization's business than does the first. This clarification is important for a number of reasons:

- Knowing where you are and stating it clearly will help you to proceed effectively with your plan.
- A clear statement of purpose is important for fund raising. Most potential donors would be "grabbed" more by the second statement, and feel that their money was supporting a worthy cause.
- It is difficult to sell or market your services without a clear definition of what they are. For public consumption, you must have clearly defined statements about your services.
- Potential consumers of your service need to know exactly what you do and how your services might differ from those of other agencies. In order to ensure access to appropriate persons, you need to clearly state whom you can help and how.
- Your staff needs a unifying concept of the organization's business and activities. It is important to know in what sort of wheel you are a cog.

As you proceed, it will be important to have a good working definition of your business that is broad enough to include all that you currently are. However, be prepared to see that definition change and expand as you move along with the planning process.

What Will Happen if We Stay in Exactly the Same Business?

In order to look at where you are to go next, it is beneficial to look at the consequences of doing nothing. What will be your organization's fate if you decide to stay exactly where you are for the next five years? Even without a crystal ball, it is possible to make some projections based on your knowledge of trends in your field. Looking back on the past five or ten years, you can probably identify trends or factors that contributed to the redefinition of your organization's business. Perhaps the growing numbers of single-parent families, an economic downturn in your service area, or an epidemic of drug abuse in the schools have significantly altered the nature of what you do or the means by which you provide your services.

Take a look at the givens in the external environment and then try to project their consequences, using any statistics, information, or "expert testimony" you may be able to gather. If your area is hard-hit by unemployment and loss of health-care benefits, the consequences of staying in a business exclusively dependent on third-party reimbursement could be disastrous. If the number of single mothers is a growing phenomenon and your father-daughter program is a major part of your organization, you could find yourself in a serious situation. By taking a look at some of your services in light of these trends, you can begin to see the need for a serious examination of your organization, its mission, and its future.

Try to identify service areas or programs that are high-risk over the next few years. This does not automatically target them for extinction; with some creative alterations or changes in market these very services can help you to come out on top. However, without identifying potential problems you could find yourself standing still and being passed by other agencies who had the foresight to be innovative and future oriented.

What Business Would We Like to Be in?

After you have carefully scrutinized your present position and areas where change is likely to be desirable, you can proceed to some creative thinking on your destination. Chances are that you and your staff already engage in periodic daydreaming about the future. Perhaps you can identify a number of new and exciting components that might be added to your program or new directions you've thought of taking. Generally, these are probably dismissed or placed on an overloaded "back burner," where they disintegrate over time.

At this point in the planning process, you can take those dreams off the shelf and give them some thought. Reality will eventually catch up with you, but the advantage of dreaming is that sometimes strategies will emerge to help those dreams come true. As a general rule, it is probably best to start out by looking at businesses related to your present services and programs. For example, a combination veterinary clinic and center for the rehabilitation of heroin addicts might have a few problems in defining and marketing its services. But there are many creative ways to redefine your business in terms that will help to build a better future.

Several examples exist of nonprofit organizations that decided to broaden the business they were in and profited by their foresight. One is the community college; rather than defining their business as providing a two-year education to high school graduates, they defined their business more comprehensively, allowing for the proliferation of adult education and informal courses, which now are a primary market and source of revenue for many community colleges. Another example of the redefinition of a business is evolving within the health-care field. Rather than retaining a narrow definition of providing in-patient care to the sick, many hospitals have stated that they are in the business of providing health care or even "wellness services." In doing so, they have broadened their markets and sources of revenue and have kept up with changing times.

By deciding what business you would like to be in, you are opening the door for your organization's growth. This does not mean that you are committed to moving in that direction tomorrow, but rather moves you closer to a long-range strategy or blueprint for growth. Perhaps there are intermediate steps or other areas to be explored along the way, but taking a hard look at what you would eventually like to do brings it a step closer to reality.

The SWOT Analysis

The SWOT analysis sounds as though it should be useful in extermination, and indeed if used properly it should enable you to exterminate some ignorance and myths about your organization. This technique calls for the examination of your organization's *strengths, weaknesses, opportunities,* and *threats.* It is a means of exploring both your internal and external environments and coming to some conclusions about your options and issues.

The SWOT analysis can be used either as a brainstorming technique, where the group convenes and shares ideas freely, or as a written exercise to be done individually, or both. This is an exercise in which the group process can be helpful, as one idea will often lead to another. The use of a blackboard or large sheets of brown paper hung on the wall will help the group to track the process and might stimulate new ideas.

Unfortunately, it is not magic in itself, but merely a tool to gather information to be channeled into the planning process.

The first step in the SWOT analysis is to identify your organization's *strengths*. Think about all aspects of the organization. Perhaps your staff is a particular strength, or your program for retarded children. Again, attempt to be as specific as possible. What is it about your staff that makes them an organizational strength? Are they especially compassionate, hardworking, well trained, or well known in the community? What is beneficial about your program for retarded children? Is it a good program clinically, from a public relations standpoint, or does it have some unique feature? By specifically identifying your areas of strength, you begin to pinpoint possible building blocks for your organization. A reputable staff might be used to provide training at a later date, and a successful program for retarded children could spawn a counterpart for retarded adults. As in any business, it is important for a nonprofit agency to know its strengths and use them to every possible advantage. Strengths can take a number of forms:

- The organization is well managed.
- The cost-containment program has led to an excess of revenue over expenses.
- We have the largest program for adoption services in the state.
- We have an excellent speakers' bureau which has provided fantastic PR and increased referrals.
- Our physical facility is attractive.
- We have an active and growing force of volunteer workers.

Identification of strengths such as these will also serve to provide a good opportunity for giving credit where credit is due and increasing your confidence; you have done something right, and can do it again!

The identification of organizational *weaknesses* proceeds in much the same manner as the identification of strengths, and in fact can be done concurrently with the analysis of strengths; often the exploration of one will elicit ideas about the other. In defining your weaknesses, there are again a number of perspectives to be examined. Generally, your staff's perceptions of weaknesses will generate some interesting ideas. This process, however, has the potential to become threatening. While your staff is unlikely to object to hearing their programs or departments identified as strengths, identifying some aspect of the organization as a weakness can offend the person or persons who feel an ownership of the issue. It helps, again, to be as specific as possible about the nature of the weakness and avoid blanket condemnations of any part of the organization. Keeping the discussion as objective as possible should help to minimize the number of offended parties. However, the life of the organization should come first, and avoiding unpleasantries could have serious consequences when major problems remain unsolved. Weaknesses might look like this:

- We are in a tight spot financially and are limited in what we can attempt as a result.
- Our public image has been tarnished by the recent arrest of a staff member.
- We lack adequate psychiatric coverage.
- Our organization is not well known outside the small town in which we are based.
- We have had a high staff turnover, which has led to instability.
- Our organization has had difficulties responding to change.

When you have developed a list of weaknesses, scrutinize them carefully. These areas may warrant some time and attention as you proceed with your plan. Weaknesses can be minor and easily correctable, or they can require major revamping and pose a serious threat to the future of your organization. By identifying and exploring areas of weakness, you can develop plans for eliminating or working around them.

Opportunities can exist in many areas. You may already have a handle on what your organization could or should be doing in the future. Opportunities can take many forms:

- Grant money has become available to fund certain types of programs.
- A new trend or phenomenon such as cocaine addiction or eating disorders provides logical opportunities for expansion.
- The local community has a shortage of family practice physicians and may be ripe for a clinic.
- Your organization is located near an expanding, prosperous area that could be a good target for new services.
- A local agency has expressed interest in working jointly with you on the development of an innovative program.
- A rental property is available at a reasonable rate in an area you've targeted for expansion.

Identifying your opportunities allows you to plan for their becoming realities. Some of these opportunities may need to be watched over time, and others may warrant a closer look and can be assigned to a project team for a study of their feasibility. Others may not be worth any further attention, and can be dismissed. Here, the arts of planning and management prevail. Your staff's perspectives and input can prove exceedingly valuable as you proceed.

Threats are generally external, although occasionally there may be a situation within your organization that poses a threat. If you suspect embezzlement of funds, that is certainly a threat from within, but it is not a long-range planning issue! Most threats relate to circumstances that may prove harmful to your organization in the near or distant future. They might include:

- A new organization is opening across the street that is targeting your clients as its customers.
- A proposed cutback of the federal funds on which several of your programs depend.
- The changing demographics of your area indicate that there will no longer be many young people to utilize your recreation program within five years.
- The declining economy in your county has resulted in a 25 percent reduction in donations over the last two years.
- Proposed accreditation regulations will mean more paperwork and less direct service time for your staff.
- A pro-life group is picketing your women's health service and intimidating your clients.

Threats such as these can hold major consequences to your organization if they are not addressed. Attempting to anticipate threats can help you to prepare for them, and can help you to budget for changes in funding or utilization of services. Planning for eventual threats can also help you to fight back—to explore new sources of grant money or other revenue, to change your target population, or to move to a new location. Ignoring threats is a dangerous business; hopefully we can learn to shoot, retreat, or regroup before we see the whites of their eyes!

Do not expect or attempt consensus as you carry out the SWOT analysis. It is a sign of a good process if a number of different ideas are generated. It should also not be surprising if the participants in the analysis do not agree. Each person comes to the planning process with a unique viewpoint based on his or her position in the organization, length of service, personality, and outlook on life. Two staff members might see the same aspect of your organization very differently; one as a strength, and the other as a weakness. This disagreement might reflect different perspectives, and it may also mirror reality; there are times when an organization's biggest strength is also its major weakness. For example, a very popular educational program for underprivileged children is losing money on a daily basis. Educational specialists and the controller might label this program as a strength and a weakness, respectively, and both would be correct. Eliciting this kind of information as concretely as possible can prove valuable, although it may be uncomfortable and produce raised eyebrows at the time.

The completion of the SWOT analysis is one rather comprehensive tool for examining your organization both in terms of its internal structure and operations and its position in the overall environment. Issues discovered at this stage can become fodder for planning groups, or can be earmarked for exploration at a later date; clearly it is impossible to do an exhaustive review of every issue relevant to the organization. Hopefully, the concept of analyzing your strengths, weaknesses, opportunities, and threats will become an ongoing part of your planning and management activities. Such a list is never static and is subject to rapid and frequent change.

Environmental Scanning

Environmental scanning describes the process of looking at the world around you. As in the identification of threats and opportunities, it is geared to the analysis of external data. There are a number of factors that affect your operation, and identifying them can be a helpful step in planning your response to circumstances that help to control your destiny. Environmental scanning probably already occurs informally on an ongoing basis within your organization. On a formal basis, it can be beneficial to look carefully at factors that have an impact on the following areas:

Economic. The realities of funding, the economic condition and climate of your area, and reimbursement issues all fall into this category. The economic realities cannot be ignored in the development of a strategic plan.

Legal or regulatory. Changes in laws or the regulations applying to society or nonprofits can have a major impact. Changes in the Medicare system, accreditation standards, drunk driving laws, and child abuse reporting regulations can have a major impact on an organization's operations, potential markets, and funding.

Political. The political environment can be influenced by nonprofit agencies and their constituencies; lobbying efforts can be successful, and the development of an awareness of the workings and events of the political system can help an organization to be aware of changes that are on the way.

Technological or medical. The development of new drugs to treat mental illness, advancements in equipment for the disabled, and new diagnostic procedures are examples of changes in technology that can impact nonprofits. Keeping abreast of new developments can allow your organization to be at the forefront of new ideas, and can help you to provide the best, most up-to-date service to your clients.

Social. An awareness of social realities is essential to nonprofit, people-oriented businesses. Higher divorce rates, more open acknowledgement of homosexuality, two-career families, and latchkey children are only a few of the trends that will have an affect on many nonprofit organizations. These social phenomena will govern to some extent how you operate, what services are needed, and who your market might be.

Demographic. A knowledge of who is out there will help you to gear your services accordingly and better define your market. Getting a handle on the demographics of your clientele and the general population in your area can yield some interesting information concerning your appeal and reputation. Demographics also help you to determine a possible demand for services, and can pinpoint promising locations for expansion.

Competitive. Identifying and compiling data on your competitors is a vital part of strategic planning, and will be explored in some depth in the marketing chapter. Knowing who your competitors are is a first step in increasing your market share.

Environmental scanning is a means whereby your organization can systematically examine and compile data on a number of factors that will be significant to you now and in the future. Again, centralizing information on these factors can help you to understand and investigate the realities that will play a major role in the development of your strategic plan.

Identifying the Givens

In any organization, there are a number of elements that are not open to change. To minimize wheel-spinning and to understand the implications of these realities, you will need to identify what they are. Since strategic planning involves looking at fundamental issues, it is important to know how fundamental your analysis can be.

Givens might exist because of limits imposed on the organization externally or by the choice of those who set the policies and philosophy by which the organization lives. For example, an agency that is part of the state human resources department is limited in terms of its funding and corporate control; it would have a difficult time becoming an independent agency and ignoring state wage scales and guidelines. Likewise, hospitals must abide by detailed operating standards in order to be accredited and receive third-party reimbursement. Some of the givens do limit our creativity, but can also challenge it. Knowing that there is little control over factors important to your operation can be frustrating, but if this is an issue in your organization, it may help to explore what those limits actually are and whether you have any flexibility within the framework of that reality.

Some of the givens are imposed by the organization and are fundamental to that agency's identity. An osteopathic hospital has a clearly defined operating philosophy and employs osteopathic physicians. An alcoholism program may be based on the Alcoholics Anonymous model of recovery and espouse total abstinence from mind-altering drugs. A women's health clinic that provides family planning services may choose to assume a pro-choice position on the issue of abortion. These are all very fundamental issues for these organizations; any shift in these philosophies would radically alter the structure and mission of the organization. There are times when such shifts are warranted; perhaps some of your fundamental assumptions are now open to question due to changes within the organization or in the external environment. By defining these givens, you define your identity and areas that are basic to the organization's existence.

Sacred Cows

Nearly every organization keeps a few sacred cows hidden away somewhere. Their size and number vary, but their impact is almost always felt. Clues to the presence of sacred cows can include statements such as:

- "But we've always done it this way!"
- "Joe has worked here for twenty years and has always run our men's group on Wednesday nights."
- "I know that program is losing money and has been poorly utilized, but the director is invested in it."
- "How could we possibly add a class for slow learners? Our staff is not qualified and we always fill these slots from within."

The common thread in these statements is an irrational entrenchment in the past and maintaining the status quo. Many organizations avoid boat-rocking at all costs, allowing sacred cows to thrive at the expense of the greater good. Identifying sacred cows is risky because of their status, and may take a fair amount of courage. Asking gentle but pointed questions about these assumptions may help to flush out irrational or outdated assumptions and subject them to closer scrutiny. Suggesting that a closer look be taken may initially be viewed as an act of heresy, but it may yield to a productive discussion. Even if the conclusion is to allow the sacred cow a long and happy life, recognizing this limitation is useful knowledge as your proceed with your plan.

CORPORATE IDENTITY ISSUES

Once you have analyzed, scrutinized, and itemized, the next step is to summarize. What have you learned about your organization, about who you are and what you do? The development of specific, written statements of corporate identity help to define your organization to your staff, stakeholders, donors, and the public who will hopefully be aware of your existence.

The Mission Statement

Every nonprofit should have a mission—a reason for being and doing what you do. The mission statement is a way of capsulizing in understandable form the reasons why your organization exists. While you may have several volumes of technical, indecipherable policy and procedure manuals, the mission statement captures the essence or unifying concept of the organization.

Having a mission statement is important in differentiating your organization from all the others, and can serve as a cornerstone for your corporate planning. It is important to reexamine your mission statement if you already have one, or to develop one if you do not.

Looking back at your statements regarding the businesses you are in and would like to be in is a good starting point for the development of your corporate mission. Try to develop a mission statement that both describes what you do and allows room for anticipated growth and movement if possible. All your activities should fall within the realm of your statement. If your mission is to provide volunteer management assistance to small businesses, how do you explain your program for assisting the elderly with income tax returns? A good mission statement will encompass your services and programs in a way that is broad enough to be inclusive but narrow enough to be meaningful. "We help people" might cover most nonprofits, but gives us no information to distinguish one from another, and fails to help us know if we should go to this agency for financial assistance or the amputation of a hangnail.

A good mission statement should not exceed the limits of the human memory. If your staff cannot repeat it with a little prompting, it is probably too long or complicated. Mission statements will hopefully have an element of zinginess, and may be useful for marketing, fund raising, or creating public awareness. The development of a solid mission statement is an exercise in creativity and might be fodder for a brainstorming session or a contest.

Knowing what your mission is can help you to clearly articulate what your programs consist of and to respond to questions about your organization. The ability to say, "Smalltown Clinic is an organization dedicated to the prevention and treatment of stress-related illnesses in a drug-free environment" allows you to succinctly explain and easily understand what you are in business to do. It's a great deal different from saying, "Well, we help people with nervous conditions feel better."

Corporate Values and Philosophy

Why do you do what you do the way you do it? This complicated question might have a number of complicated answers, which hopefully will relate in most cases to your corporate philosophy. Smalltown Clinic does not prescribe valium for stress-related illnesses, because of a fundamental belief that drugs do not resolve stressors in the best way possible. It is not because they lack physicians to prescribe the drug, because valium is expensive, or because the nearest pharmacy is several miles away. The decision is made for reasons of corporate values and philosophy.

Having a well-defined, written philosophy statement provides backing to the mission statement. It explains the reasons behind the mission statement and defines the fundamental beliefs of the organization. A nurse who believes that valium is a wonder drug in dealing with stress and a patient who is looking for a prescription would not be happy at Smalltown Clinic. This clearly stated philosophy will save both parties time and aggravation if they read and believe it, and endeavor to either find an organization that will better suit their needs or decide to be flexible enough to give the drug-free approach a try.

Hopefully your philosophy will serve as a unifying force for your staff and stakeholders. It also gives a clear message to the outside world about your commitment to what you do. Within the for-profit world, McDonald's has been recognized for their brief, repeatable statement of corporate values: Q.S.C.V.—Quality, Service, Cleanliness and Value. This simple statement provides the basis for corporate priorities and actions, and can serve as a powerful public relations tool as well.

While your philosophy may lack the simple appeal of the hamburger world, you can try to communicate as clearly as possible what is important to you. This philosophy, once developed, deserves a prominent place in your organization—in hiring and orienting staff, in promotional literature, and perhaps even in your reception area.

Corporate Charter or Bylaws

The examination of corporate documents such as the corporate charter and bylaws can be complex and require the assistance of legal counsel. Yet, they may do a great deal to define who you are. As your organization grows and evolves, a review of such documents may warrant attention. At times, these documents may require some revision and updating to reflect reality. While there may not be immediate serious consequences of being at odds with organizational bylaws, in the long run you can avoid problems if the documents are clear and not open to question. As you explore issues of corporate identity, bylaws may need reexamination or updating to keep up with the direction in which you are moving.

The Organizational Chart

Hopefully your organizational chart reflects your actual corporate structure and how your corporate structure works. If so, your task may be greatly simplified. This is an area that can cause confusion over roles, responsibilities, and relationships if it is not well defined. A related issue to be addressed is the examination of possible changes in the organizational structure as the agency follows the course that is being charted.

The subject of organizational structure is a book in itself, but several fundamental questions will need to be addressed:

• Does the present structure work?
• Are modifications needed, and if so, what form might they take?
• Do reporting relationships and departmental organization make sense?
• Where will we place new services or altered existing ones?

A poorly designed organization, like the dinosaur, could be doomed to extinction. If one department encompasses too many functions or no one is really in charge of a key area, your plans and goals may be at high risk for failure. Examination of overloads, roadblocks, and poorly designed departments can serve as the basis for significant improvement. Growing organizations, like poorly remodeled houses, can be the victims of unplanned growth, with functions added randomly, based on who has the time or is unassertive enough to assume the function. Within several years, an unwieldy structure can be the result.

Serious consideration should be given to the placement of new or evolving services within the organization. Examining your structure in terms of function, work flow, and compatibility of purpose can help you to assimilate change more smoothly. Perhaps your new service warrants another level of management, or it might be a possibility for absorption into a similar department or division. Decisions such as these can make a major impact on the eventual operation of the service.

It should be noted that it is nearly impossible to have a completely objective discussion of organizational chart issues. We all know that the Director of Adult Services is our friend Mary, and the Supervisor of the Northern Center is Joe, whom we've never cared for. Likewise, we know where we fit in and how changes might impact on us. Nevertheless, as managers we are called on to deal with difficult issues and to do the best we can.

Identification of Stakeholders

In your organizational life, as in your personal life, it is important to know who cares about you. If you have been effective in carrying forth your mission, there should be a number of people who would be affected to varying degrees if you closed shop tomorrow. Identifying these persons will help you to know both who you serve and who you can count on for funding, backing, and positive word of mouth. As mentioned earlier, a demographic analysis of your clientele is a fundamental step in the strategic planning process. Looking at this data is a logical starting point for the identification of your stakeholders, but they will undoubtedly extend beyond those you physically serve.

Stockholders in a for-profit corporation are those who are financially invested in the corporation. They will prosper through its success, and decline as a result of its failures. Stakeholders in the nonprofit sector are similar in that they are invested in your success. Naturally, the individuals who come to you for your services and programs have a stake in your survival. If they avail themselves of your services voluntarily, they would be likely to feel your loss and might be subject to the inconvenience of finding a substitute elsewhere. Stakeholders, however, include those with other forms of interest in your organization, as well.

Many families who have lost a loved one to cancer feel an investment in the success of organizations involved in cancer treatment and research. These individuals may never have come into direct contact with the organization, but might know that it provided support and information to a relative, or feel a personal commitment to the discovery of a cure for cancer. The families of patients in psychiatric treatment may develop a real investment in the work of the hospital. Women who have undergone mastectomies are often excellent volunteers in agencies that assist in coping with survival after surgery. All of these persons can be identified as sources of support for the agency's programs, whether in terms of contributions of time, money, or a positive public image.

Identifying and exploring your stakeholders can be a big boost to your success. Forming auxiliaries, advisory boards, or volunteer associations has proven helpful to many organizations in carrying out new programs, maintaining services, and raising the funds needed for operations. Knowing who cares can be a valuable asset for nonprofit organizations, many of which do not charge a fixed fee to cover the cost of their services and must count on concerned citizens for their survival. Incorporating the benefits of stakeholders into your strategic plan can help you achieve the results you are seeking.

GOAL DEVELOPMENT

As you begin to clarify some of the issues your organization is dealing with, these issues must be translated into statements of organizational goals and objectives. These goals should be made on the corporate level as well as the departmental level. While many organizations complete goals and objectives on an annual basis, it is important to understand both goals and objectives and where they fit into the planning process.

Goals are statements that describe broad, abstract intents, states, or conditions. They define the desired destination or outcome the organization is attempting to achieve. The following are examples of goals:

- We want to be the best-known hospital in our region within the next five years.
- Our goal is to cut our operating costs by 10 percent without affecting the quality of our services.
- Within three years, we want to increase the utilization of our early childhood program by 25 percent.

A clearly written goal will be specific and include time frames when possible. Just to state that your goal is to improve your services is not very informative; it would be better to state what services you will strive to improve and in what way.

An *objective* is a statement that describes specific, desired outcomes or results, and may address the actual actions or mechanisms for achieving those outcomes. Objectives are plans that are geared toward reaching identified goals. For example, a hospital whose goal is to become the best known in the region might state the following objectives:

- Increase name recognition in the next county by scheduling at least one speaker per month in that area.
- Sponsor a health fair at a local mall to familiarize the public with our programs and services.
- Develop an innovative, homelike birthing center to attract publicity and positive word of mouth from patients.

The assumption is that the achievement of these objectives will bring the hospital a step closer to the actualization of its goal of becoming better known. A clear objective will explain what you plan to do, why, and how. Specific action items may need to be added in order to clarify steps in achieving each objective, and it is important to include time frames for implementation and persons responsible for the implementation of each item. A well-written objective will be measurable; it will be easy to determine whether it has been achieved.

Clear statements of goals and objectives are important in the planning process, as they serve as vehicles for the articulation and eventually the tracking of planned courses of action.

The Superordinate Goal

A superordinate goal is a statement of the institution's primary or overriding goal. It can be somewhat general in order to encompass a number of smaller goals, but again must be specific enough so that it is meaningful. This statement can become a rallying cry for your staff, and a focal point for your activities. In developing a superordinate goal, think about the primary outcome or outcomes you hoped to achieve when you committed yourself to the development of a strategic plan. Take a look at your analysis of what business you are in and what business you want to be in; examine carefully the goals you have set to date. Any statement of goals at this point should be considered preliminary and tentative, subject to final review as the plan is developed and committed to paper.

The importance of a superordinate goal may vary from organization to organization, but having a unifying concept for your strategic and long-range plans can help to clarify your intentions and directions. The superordinate goal will deserve a prominent place in your planning document when it is developed. While each organization's superordinate goal may have a different flavor, examples might sound like this:

- To develop a regional reputation for providing residential treatment and education services to autistic children.
- To provide high-quality educational materials, training, and consultation on home safety on a national scale.
- To serve the unemployed in Home County by providing counseling, training in job-seeking skills and resume writing, and information on local job opportunities.

These superordinate goals do not necessarily describe the organization's present situation; rather, they describe the condition or state the organization hopes to achieve as a result of its planning. The agency for the unemployed mentioned above might currently have a staff of two running groups on a weekly basis to support the unemployed in Home County. However, their superordinate goal statement summarizes their intentions to develop a training program and job information bank. The details of their proposed course of action in attaining these goals would be included in their plan, developed by task forces who are digging for information and determining how the agency might best implement these plans on a practical level. The superordinate goal statement clarifies and reminds you of where you want to go.

Corporate Goals

In any but the smallest organization, there will be a need to develop goals on the corporate level, which will encompass the organization as a whole, and the departmental or divisional level, which will cover smaller functional units and support the corporate goals.

The corporate goals should be related to the achievement of the superordinate goal, and should state the priorities for the entire organization for the period covered by the plan. In the example above, corporate goals might include:

- Increase counseling efforts for the unemployed to include group, individual, and family support.
- Develop and implement a training program on resume writing and job search skills.
- Form a network of local businesses to gain information on the availability of employment opportunities.

In this case, these may be the primary goals for the organization as a whole over the next five years. To be complete, the goals would be complemented by the development of specific objectives detailing how, when, and by whom those goals are to be achieved. The goals may then be delegated to the departmental level if this is appropriate in terms of the organizational structure. If there are separate education and counseling divisions, for example, they will be responsible for the development of their respective programs.

Goals on the corporate level should set the tone for departmental goals. They should relate to the organization's mission and the furthering of its overall progress. It is on this level that reorganization, restructuring, or redefinition of the organization should occur, and issues such as these should definitely appear on the list of corporate goals. Realistically, some of these goals will remain the primary responsibility of the chief executive officer, and some will be delegated to other managers or staff.

The development of corporate goals will be greatly simplified if you have done your homework on other fundamental issues of corporate identity and structure. They will reflect these findings and conclusions, and will form a vital part of your plan for the future.

Departmental or Divisional Goals

The development of departmental goals must be related to overall corporate goals and the organization's superordinate goals. In an organization that has made a decision to phase out its program for the parents of Down's syndrome children, departmental goals should not include the hiring of an additional counselor for this purpose. The coordination of departmental with corporate goals is a real benefit of developing a systematic and well-orchestrated plan; it is important that all parts of the organization pull in the same direction.

Once overall corporate goals and directions have been developed, departmental goals should not be difficult. If a corporate goal is to develop an educational program on job-seeking skills, then the education department's goals should include plans for implementing this service, and should include detailed information on actions needed and time frames for their accomplishment. This tie-in forms a clear audit trail so that the organization can track all the components of its plan and determine their status. It also helps to avoid a sudden realization several years down the road that someone was supposed to develop a new program. In the heat of battle, it is easy to lose sight of your goals and plans for their attainment.

Departmental goals might not always relate directly to corporate goals. In the planning process, the group might come across a more effective way to provide services or a possibility of streamlining the department's operations. These discoveries are important to recognize and note; while they may not tie directly to the corporate directions, they may improve the overall functioning of the agency and therefore deserve a place in the department's goals over the next several years.

Departmental goals, however, should always be reviewed at the corporate level to determine their compatibility with the overall course of action; if implementation of the goal will cost $20,000 at a time when the corporate goal is cost-containment, further discussion and exploration may be warranted.

At the department as well as the corporate level, strategy and goal-setting are important. Especially in a large organization where departments may enjoy a degree of autonomy, it is helpful to have a framework for actions and decisions, and to chart a course for the department over a multi-year period. The development of departmental goals can help managers to manage more efficiently, to develop guidelines for operations, and to measure their performance in supporting the efforts of the organization as a whole.

Financial Goals and Plans

Depending on the needs of the organization, financial planning will assume varying degrees of importance. The picture will be different in a small agency struggling for survival than in a well-established organization with a large endowment. In either case, the development of financial plans and the consideration of financial realities will play an important part in the development of the strategic plan.

An organization for which financial issues are paramount may decide to make this area a major focus of the planning process. A task force might be formed of the financial officer, development director, and several department managers who explore financial problems and develop long-term strategy for increasing the flow of funds into the agency and wisely spending the funds available. This task might include an examination of the capability of the organization's stakeholders to increase support and the feasibility of adding new programs and services that might be revenue-producing. The development of a financial plan might extend several years into the future, and in any case must be an ongoing effort.

Financial realities must be considered in all other planning; whether a separate financial plan is developed, a hard look must be taken at the financial feasibility of proposed services, programs, and alterations in the organization's course. These must be based on as much hard data as can be mustered, including figures on past performance, revenue, and expense, and projections on future funding sources. Even a well thought-out, much-needed service can be destined for failure if financial planning is not carried out as an integral part of its development.

Depending on the sophistication of the organization's staff, outside assistance might be needed for financial planning. This is an area where the importance of good information and knowledge cannot be underestimated. The development of an accurate forecast of the financial picture is fundamental to the success of the plan. Changes in the economic picture, funding, and the impact of inflation are the subject of endless speculation by high-level experts, and can be difficult for a small organization to project. However, a thorough exploration of the past, present, and possible future scenarios must be undertaken in the development of a workable plan.

Fund-Raising Goals and Plans

An important part of the development of a strategic plan is an examination of the organization's ability to fund its projects and programs. As part of the formulation of a long-range funding strategy, fund-raising issues will play an important role.

Nonprofit organizations almost invariably rely on donations from outside sources to fund or subsidize their programs and services. The flow of this funding, however, is generally not under the direct control of the organization, and is subject to conditions of the economy, regulatory changes, and the whims of donors. Building a stable base of donors is an essential part of nonprofit management, and one that requires long-term commitment. Whether development efforts are low-key volunteer activities or the domain of fund-raising professionals in your organization, the integration of fund-raising issues into the strategic plan is vital.

Identification of stakeholders, addressed earlier, is a good tool for identifying potential donors. Also, you may need to do some homework to learn about foundations and corporations in your area with which you may not already be familiar. Find out what sort of interests they express and what projects they have funded in the past. Familiarize yourself with key personnel within those organizations, and look for contact points through your staff, board of directors, and committed stakeholders. By learning more about potential donors, you can secure valuable input into your planning process. This can assist you in determining whether there is a potential for a startup grant for a new service, or in discovering what programs are fundable, and molding your plans to fit that reality.

A long-term fund-raising strategy might consist of the development of an annual or regular appeal, giving programs for designated services, and the establishment of a centralized source of information within your organization on local foundations. By learning to tap these sources, you may greatly expand your prospects for success.

Setting clear-cut goals in the area of development is also possible and desirable within the framework of the long-range plan. While you will undoubtedly take whatever donations you can get, it helps to begin placing some realistic expectations on those donations based on past history, available figures from similar organizations, and the expectations you have for the success of your new approaches. Goal-setting is a good way of measuring the success of your plans, and will help you to project your needs over a multi-year period. Donations totaling $50,000 can be a measure of success or failure, depending on your needs, goals, and the amount of time and money required to raise them.

The development of a strategic plan can also assist you in knowing the direction your agency will take, which will significantly aid your ability to appeal for funding. Having a clear direction can help you convince potential donors of the importance of their part in your efforts, and can help to give them a better idea of what they are funding. While appealing to the emotions of donors is an undeniable factor in giving, the presence of a well thought-out plan to deal with little children or homeless adults will place your appeal on more solid ground.

4

The Process of Planning

The pessimist sees the difficulty in every opportunity; the
optimist, the opportunity in every difficulty.

L. P. Jacks

Your organization, like all others, undoubtedly faces a number of
difficulties as well as opportunities. Your task during the planning process is to identify both and work toward creating pluses out of minuses.
This is not an easy task; it requires vision, hard work, business savvy,
and the coordinated efforts of a number of people. As in most projects,
the manner in which you approach the planning process can contribute
significantly to its success or failure.

Any project that involves the collective labor of a group of people has
the potential to work smoothly or become unwieldy. While your staff
may have acquired the decency not to sail paper airplanes at meetings,
a well-structured agenda and approach to your planning sessions can
help boost productivity and help the process on its way.

Strategic planning, more than many of the undertakings in the life of
an organization, is process oriented. Because it requires the commitment,
expertise, and efforts of so many staff members on all levels, it is important to build in some regard for the cast of characters and remember
that one of the important by-products of planning can be increased
cohesiveness and commitment of staff. Moving carefully and strategically through the process can help you to achieve your desired results.

Strategic planning may differ from other management activities within the organization in that the issues are not as obvious and well defined. Especially in an organization geared to crisis management, the emphasis is on responding to immediate issues that impact on the daily operations of the organization. It is much easier to identify and deal with such issues; often there is little choice unless the organization is willing to fall into a haphazard pattern of making yesterday's decisions tomorrow. In strategic planning, we are identifying and dealing with issues that may not be of such obvious or immediate importance. They are likely to be fuzzier and represent a style of thinking and operating with which the organization's personnel is not familiar. For these reasons, it is especially important to carefully plan each step of the operation to achieve desired results. While a decision to cut this year's budget to avoid a deficit may be clear-cut and immediate, a decision to begin a fund-raising campaign in two years will require a different perspective and approach.

PLANNING AND HOLDING EFFECTIVE MEETINGS

While strategic planning requires the collection of statistics and information, the basis of their usefulness is in their interpretation and ideas on how those facts might best be used. To that end, it helps to plan your meetings well. For optimum efficiency, your staff will appreciate an opportunity to know what is happening today, and how they might best prepare.

A vital tool in achieving this preparation is the agenda. A well thought-out agenda can help to break the group's task into manageable chunks and help them to clarify their goals. If the day's agenda is the examination of demographic data to determine the best location for the new office, the staff can review the data and do some thinking about the issue in preparation for the discussion. The issue of the new office is undoubtedly only one step in the development of a larger project, such as the startup of a new service. By looking at one component at a time in a logical sequence, the overwhelming global tasks can be broken down into their component parts and addressed one by one. This not only improves efficiency, but boosts morale as the group records its accomplishment in tackling well-defined tasks as well as moving toward its ultimate goal.

Consultation with committee members prior to the meeting can help you to develop an effective agenda, especially if the group is starting a new project or going in a new direction. This helps to foster involvement in the project, may generate new ideas and approaches to the issue, and can help to minimize surprises. To call a meeting of a group whose purpose is to develop a long-term funding strategy and have a member announce, "I think this whole idea is stupid" can be quite a shock. By checking with members prior to the meeting, you can be better prepared to deal with their issues and still carry through the mission of the group.

Circulating agendas and materials ahead of the meeting date can minimize the time wasted on extraneous issues, and can help the group get down to business. Some questions might be addressed prior to the meeting, and a review of pertinent information can precede the discussion. Setting goals for each meeting helps you to know what you need to accomplish, and tells you when the meeting is over. Naturally, some carryover of items from one meeting to another may occur if there is a legitimate need for more information or if the issue is more heated or complex than anticipated.

STYLE AND SUBSTANCE IN MEETING FORMATS

Giving some thought to the format of meetings is also worthwhile. Considerations such as the length and location of the meeting and the manner in which the discussion will be approached can make a big difference in the success of your undertaking. While the discussion of a well-defined, concrete issue such as the location of a new office might be straightforward and time-limited, the exploration of a more complex issue such as what business you are in will warrant a different type of preparation and discussion.

The occasional availability of an off-site meeting place can be a real advantage to the planning process for a number of reasons:

- Interruptions by phone calls, people barging in, and staff members suddenly remembering important duties will be minimized.
- The site can represent "neutral territory" when hot political or turf issues are under consideration.
- A fresh setting can help with a fresh perspective.
- If desired, the meeting can be casual and informal. Participants can be asked to wear their jeans, and shed their working hours inhibitions and mentality in the process.
- Staff who are working hard can feel rewarded by a change of scenery, a day away from the office, and perhaps a free meal. Good morale may contribute to good thinking.

Scheduling a meeting at a local hotel, school, or even at the home of a generous staff member should be considered, especially for issues that require a great deal of time, processing, and creativity. For those who can afford it, a retreat of several days' duration can prove immensely helpful, especially during the startup and windup of the planning process. Again, this contributes to morale and teamwork while providing a reward for effort above and beyond the call of duty.

Giving some thought to the way the meeting will be conducted will help to set the stage, whether your meeting is at your facility or off-site. The use of creative strategies can help your meeting to move more smoothly. Depending on the issue, the cast of characters, and the setting, varying degrees of informality may be appropriate. If your chief executive would rather die than loosen up in front of the staff, you may not want to use a warm-up technique where everyone is asked to imitate a favorite animal. On the other hand, sometimes a warm-up exercise can help a group shed inhibitions and facilitate a free exchange of ideas.

BRAINSTORMS AND BEYOND

Creative thinking is a vital ingredient of a successful planning process. Yet creativity can be achieved by a group of starchy executives in three-piece suits as readily as by a bunch of jeans-clad staffers sitting on the floor. The ability to have a useful brainstorm is important, but of equal importance is the ability to take the results a step beyond into useful, reality-based thinking.

Techniques such as storyboarding, in which ideas are called out and placed on a board according to category, can be extremely useful in the planning process. This technique can help you to organize your thoughts on a topic or group of related topics, such as identifying possible names for a new service or trying to think of all the components to planning an open house. By listing all the categories, such as personnel and staffing, refreshments, possible dates, program, and speakers, you can develop a number of ideas for an effective open house. Any technique that lends itself to creativity and organization might be used.

Traditional brainstorming techniques can also be useful; your staff can be asked to think of ideas for marketing your program for working women, and can call out all the possibilities, regardless of how absurd they may seem. This technique is useful in that it does not censor ideas that may seem absurd but hold merit on closer examination. This type of group thinking also promotes "hitchhiking," in which one person can expand on or slightly alter another's idea. Holding a rummage sale to raise funds may be a terrible idea for your organization, which is attempting to upgrade its image. However, an antique sale whose proceeds are donated might help to raise funds while lending a classier image to your organization. "Hitchhiking" can provide added ingredients or twists that can turn a bad idea into a good one, or improve an idea from good to fantastic. The collective wisdom of your planning group should not be underestimated.

Relatively unstructured thinking can be fun, stimulating, and can infuse some enthusiasm into what can be a difficult process. However, the step beyond brainstorming techniques is crucial. Building the link between fantasy and reality can be difficult, and not nearly so much fun. Developing good, creative ideas is not an end in itself. For every creative activity, there must be an equal number of activities devoted to the drudgework of reality. Translating creative ideas into practical tactics requires an organized, planned approach. It is possible to develop wonderfully attractive, creative approaches that also hold no basis in reality. For example, a structured in-patient program for gamblers might be an excellent idea, but if insurance companies will not reimburse for such a program, and the gamblers by definition have no money since losses and not wins will motivate them for treatment, how good is the idea?

Taking the brainstorming process one step further, examining the pros and cons and feasibility of ideas is a necessary tactic in the development of a strategic plan. Working creatively within the bounds of reality can be a juggling act, but it is a step that cannot be skipped.

INVOLVING STAFF AND THE BOARD IN THE PROCESS

Since one of the fringe benefits of strategic planning can be heightened enthusiasm and cohesiveness for your staff and board of directors, be careful not to miss this opportunity to involve them in the planning process. Their involvement can be valuable for several reasons; they will feel more a part of the process, and may contribute some valuable ideas or variations to the development of the plan.

There are several ways that staff can be pulled into the process:

• Questionnaires can be circulated to the staff, soliciting their input on key issues identified by the planning group. Asking their opinion on the best way to raise needed funds or market services might yield some interesting information. Perhaps someone knows Mr. Moneybags, the local millionaire, and thinks he may be willing to donate. Another staffer's aunt may own the town newspaper and be persuaded to do a feature story on your efforts. Or maybe someone will simply come up with a new, creative idea. Although not everyone is likely to respond, the input given may be valuable and everyone enjoys feeling important enough to be considered.

• Brainstorming or information-gathering sessions can be held with selected groups of staff members. If a key topic under consideration is the future of the program for visually disabled children, talking to the teachers, aides, and therapists who work in that program each day may tell you more than the administrator or the statistics can communicate. They may be able to pinpoint problems and develop suggestions that are right on target, but nobody ever asked before; their expertise in their area is a resource too valuable to ignore. Making changes in a service is also easier politically if those involved have been consulted and feel that they own a part of the decision. Gaining support for the plan cannot be underestimated as part of the process.

• Information sessions can be held with staff as the plan proceeds. Periodic meetings with staff in small groups or as a whole can be used to communicate preliminary thoughts and plans. This serves to demystify the process for those who do not live with it daily, draws them closer, and again affords an opportunity for their input.

In dealing with staff, it is important to keep in mind the sensitivity of some of the material you are exploring. Perhaps you will not want to announce a major change in the direction of the agency until it is thought through by key people in order to avoid the panic and insecurity that inevitably accompany change. Casually mentioning the consideration of eliminating your group for juvenile offenders will not do much for the morale of those employed by that program, and may send shock waves throughout the organization. Prudence in sharing information is definitely warranted.

It is important, whatever mechanism you choose, that because of their involvement, your staff feels that they are informed and listened to. Even ridiculous ideas should be greeted with courtesy; "That's an interesting idea" is probably true in most cases, and is an acceptable comment to an idea that is naive or on an erroneous track. Remember that one of your primary goals is to have your staff leave saying, "Gee, this is an exciting time to be a part of this organization!" or at least something fairly similar.

Involving the board of directors also requires some finesse. Individual meetings may be warranted with some members, especially where controversial ideas or major change are involved. Their opinions will matter when you move toward approval of the plan, so anticipating their reactions and dealing with problems is an important step.

Techniques similar to those listed above can be used to solicit the directors' input and stimulate their involvement. Whether you choose to deal with board members individually, in small groups, or as a whole, try to keep in mind their primary concerns. They may show more interest in the bottom line and break-even points, or may be interested in the social aspect of a service, depending on their backgrounds. Try to prepare for likely questions; doing your homework will help you to be effective in strategic planning at the board level.

Periodic presentations on the plan's progress to the board of directors will serve to inform them as plans are developed, and will minimize or eliminate surprises later in the process. Boards keep sacred cows as well, so being aware of their realities will ensure a smoother process.

DEALING WITH PROBLEMS AND PITFALLS IN THE PROCESS

Due to the fact that your staff is only human, there are a number of roadblocks to watch out for as you proceed with your plan. A number of human elements will arise, which will both enrich and interfere with the process of mapping out your organization's future. Anticipating and being able to deal with these issues will make you an effective planner.

Creative Conflict

Fighting makes some people very nervous, and can be construed as a sign of imminent disaster. Fair, clean fighting, in fact, can be a sign of organizational health. Totally avoiding conflict and attempting premature consensus can lead to far worse results than the occasional friendly brawl.

Any time fundamental issues are discussed by people with an investment in their outcome, disagreement is likely to result. You are in serious trouble only if opposing factions attempt to turn the situation into an "us against them" war. Short of that, it is a challenge to the skills of the group's facilitator to clarify issues and attempt to discuss the basic areas of conflict. Also, it is possible that two people who agree can have a heated argument without realizing that their differences are merely semantic or a difference in framework or perspective. A good leader will work toward helping the participants to pinpoint areas of disagreement, and determine a course of action for their resolution.

Planning is not group therapy, nor is the ancestry of the participants in question. Personal vendettas should be cut off, and the discussion should be refocused to relevant matters. At the other extreme, underlying issues may need to be drawn out; for example, a participant's concern for the welfare of her clients or the future of her job may be behind her hostility on the issue of changes in an existing service. By identifying the root of the concern, it may be possible to move closer to appropriate action.

Planning would probably be dull, unstimulating, and unproductive if everyone agreed on every issue. The integrity of your staff and your organization could then be called into question. Use conflict as an indicator that there may be several valid perspectives on the topic in question, and a guide to areas that warrant further exploration.

Initial Drops in Morale

You may ask, if the development of a strategic plan is so great, why your staff's morale has actually dropped in the initial stages of planning. There are a number of reasons this might occur:

- They are already overworked and can't imagine taking on one more thing.
- They remain unconvinced of the usefulness of planning; your task will be to work with them to see its merits or push them along until they get moving.

- They are overwhelmed by the scope of the project and haven't been able to look at it in manageable components.
- They are threatened by the prospect of change in a comfortable environment.

An assessment of causes will be the first step to the discovery of the cure. It may help to give the staff adequate information on what is being done and why, as well as to individually address their specific concerns and helping to understand the potential benefits of their programs and services. Point out to them the opportunity to deal with issues they want to see addressed. Staff may need reassurance about other responsibilities that they see as more pressing. By all means, however, give them the clear message that this is important and worthwhile. Try to develop a sense of commitment early in the process, so that staff will have the energy to proceed in spite of the workloads of their "regular jobs."

Confidentiality and Responsibility Issues

The participants in the strategic planning process are charged with an important responsibility; good strategic thinking and the development of a workable plan can be the keys to the organization's survival and growth. Here, as in many management tasks, the staff's sense of responsibility is an important ingredient. Speaking to staff regarding lackadaisical attitudes is worthwhile; lack of commitment and responsibility in the process warrants attention. Another important issue is the ability to keep the planning activities appropriately confidential. You probably do not want to make public announcements to your competitors about your preliminary plans so that your ideas can be borrowed. Also, there may be sensitive issues that are not appropriate for discussion with the entire staff. Attention to these facts can avoid some very sticky problems. If a discussion is to be kept confidential, say so and mean it. Minutes do not need to be circulated at all times, and reports on sensitive issues can be read and then collected at the meeting. Even the Pentagon has leaks, so your organization is not safe from the premature or badly timed dissemination of sensitive information. However, taking every precaution to prevent leaky planning is worth the effort.

Loners and Resistance to the Process

Nearly every organization has them—individuals who may be dynamite workers, who are loyal and dedicated, but who have no sympathy for the importance of group process. This type of employee may be entrepreneurial, a rugged individualist, arrogant, shy, or staunchly of the belief that the best way to approach a task is simply to go do it. Pulling the loner into the process can range from difficult to impossible, yet it is a necessary step to a successful plan, especially if the loner holds a key position.

Resistance to the planning process may also reflect feelings of being threatened or left out, or a lack of commitment to the organization. In any case, it is important to attempt to pull outsiders into the process. Techniques for doing this may vary and can include giving an important assignment, talking with the loner individually about the importance of his contribution, soliciting comments in meetings if they are not offered spontaneously, and enlisting the support of respected colleagues in wooing the reluctant party. Realistically, not every person is a team player, and some very important assets can exist in an otherwise standoffish employee. As plans for the organization are developed, however, every staff member should be made to feel a part of those plans to the extent possible. Identifying and attempting to deal with issues of resistance can serve as an insurance policy against lack of cooperation or of commitment as the organization moves to implement its plans.

Subtle Sabotage

Some of the most interesting parts of organizational life take place informally, behind closed doors. Perhaps one of the most discouraging experiences in planning is reaching an apparent conclusion or consensus, only to discover later that a member of the "team" is secretly disgruntled or dissatisfied and happy to share it with others. Healthy conflict and clean fighting can actually prove beneficial to the planning process, but there is a certain destructiveness to subtle sabotage.

The dynamics of subtle sabotage are usually born in the hearts of one or two individuals who either fail to speak their minds, or do not feel satisfied with the results when they do. Their next course of action is to attempt, in small ways, to stack the deck against the recommendations of others. By continually planning counterattacks or whispering campaigns, or simply ignoring the mainstream, subtle saboteurs can throw quite a monkey wrench into the planning process.

Sabotage can rear its ugly head either during the planning process, as an effort is mounted to prevent a certain course of action, or during the implementation of the plan. In either case, it is wise to attempt to bring it out in the open. By stating, "Lucy, I get the feeling you don't agree with what this committee is recommending," or "I understand you have some concerns about this project, and I'd like to hear about them," you begin the process of bringing the underground above ground. It's possible that the saboteur has some legitimate concerns or good ideas once the element of negativity has been stripped away. Also, dealing with these concerns openly may help the alienated staff member to feel more a part of the process or at least to feel she has been listened to and understood. This in itself may begin to dissipate the anger.

Most organizations are not democracies; someone is in charge and must ultimately take responsibility for making decisions. However, the support of the staff is a most valuable asset, and lack of support can spell serious problems for the organization's plans. It is worth the discomfort and detours to attempt to deal with issues in a straightforward fashion in order to prevent dealing with them in indirect ways for years to come.

Turf and Power Issues

Even very nice people can turn ugly when issues of power and territory are at stake. Civilization has not removed from us ancient urges to protect what is ours at all costs. You will undoubtedly be reminded of this quirk of human nature the first time you tread on the territory of another in the development of the strategic plan.

Unfortunately, there is no simple solution to the turf problem. Unless you are starting with all new staff, every piece of the organization "belongs" to someone, and invading that ownership can be threatening. Most people will also welcome an opportunity to expand their own territory, and may be less than ecstatic when a colleague's territory expands even more. If you aren't careful, you could avoid dealing with the turf of the individual whose growl is most threatening and teeth look the sharpest.

Attempting to be as objective and supportive as possible is probably the best approach to territoriality in most situations. Communicating that a program or approach is outmoded is always difficult, but may be softened some by an indication of the positive functions it has served in the past and a simple statement of the facts, which lead to the unfortunate conclusion that changes must be made to support the organization's strategy. Sometimes speaking with key people individually can help to defuse hot turf issues, as can helping them see the beneficial as well as the threatening sides of change.

It is difficult to deal with turf and power issues completely objectively. If you are developing a new program that might logically fit better under the related domain of Manager X, but you know Manager Y has better skills to make it succeed, who do you favor for the expanded turf? If Manager Z is bright and capable but prone to bragging and ruthlessness with those less powerful, do you favor him for expanded responsibilities over Manager Q, who is a heck of a nice guy and very cooperative but considerably less skilled? Staffs are made up of collections of imperfect people, nearly all of whom would like to get ahead, and many of whom will favor the plans that will serve to advance their personal and professional interests.

Inherent in strategic planning is the promise of growth and change. This condition may serve to awaken the latent ambition and territoriality in even the most sedate of staff members. Imagine, if you will, an orderly crowd milling peacefully about. Then imagine the behavior of that crowd if suddenly an airplane passes overhead and drops a load of dollar bills down into the crowd. The crowd will undoubtedly become less orderly as each person scrambles for a share of the riches. While some may be content with a few dollar bills, others may not be content until they have seized all the money in the vicinity. Riots have broken out with less provocation. On a smaller scale, the strategic planning process can create a similar scenario. Growth implies an increase in the available territory and accompanying power. While ego and power issues may have been dormant due to a relatively stable situation in the organization, when there is the possibility of expansion people come charging forward to claim a share. Again, exact behavior will depend on the cast of characters; in some organizations people will be exceedingly civilized about it, and in others a brawl may occur in reaching for fame and glory.

Lest this sounds too negative, there is a positive side to the power motive in that it can move people toward greater productivity. Ambition and the entrepreneurial spirit are admirable characteristics, so long as they do not run rampant and become powerful forces that disrupt a relatively orderly progression toward the common good. Your organization could have just as much trouble with a weak and uninspired staff as with a staff fighting for turf and power. Strong leadership within the organization can strike a balance between power issues and organizational goals, and can use the strength and ambition of the staff in a manner that is beneficial to both.

The informal structure of an organization is made up of clusters and subgroups not reflected on the organizational chart. These alliances will undoubtedly play a part in the planning process, and can even help contribute to getting things done. They can also be obstructions to the task at hand. By working with these groups to draw them into the process and attempting to make their thoughts public, you can try to work toward a more unified approach. Again, the important factor is keeping the needs of the organization firmly in mind and clearly communicating priorities to the staff involved.

Role Conflict in Small Organizations

As we discussed in Chapter 1, in large organizations the top managers are likely to set strategy, the middle managers will develop tactics for carrying out strategy, and lower-level managers will oversee the operations of the corporation intended to support strategy and tactics. In this structure, for example, the top executives can decide that for the next five years automotive manufacturing will concentrate on the production of smaller cars, the middle layer will develop the plans for the cars, and the lower layer will supervise the manufacture of the small cars mandated by top management. Everyone knows (approximately) his or her place, and the lower-level managers know that they cannot force top managers to return to larger cars simply because they are more familiar to the workers and supervisors. Therefore, the organization changes from the top down, based on trends, forecasts, and the recommendations of those knowledgeable about the auto industry.

In small nonprofit organizations the scenario is likely to be different. Top, middle, and lower levels of management may all be the same people, who are responsible for mandating, implementing, and sweating out any and all changes. Here, the situation is not so clean. Top management will not only set the strategy of the organization, they must also know it intimately from the inside out. There are advantages to this; the people involved are well aware of the practical realities that face the organization. However, it is also more tempting to resist change because of the difficulty associated with implementing it.

The goal in strategic planning is to remain as firmly fixed as possible on issues of organizational strategy; the development of tactics and operational plans will come later. Attempting to focus consistently on strategy issues will be quite a chore. When a member of your staff begins thinking, "Oh, no! We can't develop an evening program because Millie always likes to go home before 4:30 and she'll threaten to quit if I ask her to work late!" you are definitely experiencing a case of role conflict. The overall good of the organization could possibly be compromised in favor of the avoidance of dealing with Millie. Can you imagine top executives in the auto industry saying, "We can't make small cars this year because Joe Smith on the assembly line would need to learn a new job, and he doesn't want to"? Yet this type of thinking can creep into small, humanistic organizations and prevent healthy growth and change.

It is a tribute to the nonprofit manager that he or she is versatile and able to manage on several levels at once. Perhaps in a small organization with limited resources the tactical and operational details will render a strategy unwieldy or impossible. However, don't abandon potentially promising directions simply because of the fear of problems on lower levels. Pursue them as vigorously as possible at the strategic level before convincing yourself that change is too difficult to live with.

Growing Pains and Sentimental Journeys

Strategic planning, for many organizations, will spell growth and change. Growing pains can be frightening to a small, homey agency where everyone knows everyone and "it's always been this way." The mention of change or growth can give way to waves of nostalgia and a fear of the future.

To some nonprofit organizations, the strategic planning process will force staff to face realities with which they are unfamiliar or to which they are unaccustomed. Discussing concepts such as market shares, break-even points, and business plans may be antithetical to their view of the organization as a humanistic, people-oriented, service organization. The change may be threatening or uncomfortable to the extent that it challenges beliefs or brings into focus a view that is unfamiliar. Yet staffs in nonprofit organizations are increasingly faced with the realities of the business world, and must deal in the realm of dollars and cents.

Your staff may need some reassurance that you are not abandoning your interest in serving the needs of others. A statement or reaffirmation of your corporate values should occur through your mission and philosophy, and staff members will need to know that this mission is still your organization's reason for being. Helping to explode the myth that nonprofit status equals poverty and familiarizing your staff with the concept of the profitable nonprofit will pave the way for their acceptance of change, although it will not occur overnight. Since your profits do not line the pockets of private individuals, your motivation for change undoubtedly does revolve around better service, smoother operations, and ultimately the survival of your organization and its ability to carry forth its mission. Although some old-timers may grow misty-eyed reminiscing about the day the office first opened with two staff members and a secretary, they also need your help to get in touch with and keep up with the march of time.

Problems in Reaching a Consensus

You sit down, review the data, discuss your options, and quickly conclude that it's time to broaden your idea of your business to include two new concepts. Once agreed, you move on and begin to develop plans for implementing your newly adopted strategy.

The above is an ideal scenario that may or may not actually happen in your organization. It is possible that the reality is so obvious or your staff is all on such a similar wavelength that a consensus emerges quickly and with no dissent. However, it is also at least equally likely that it will not be that simple. For reasons of turf, different perspectives, unstated alliances, or who knows what else, your staff may experience serious, fundamental disagreements.

What do you do when nine of the ten members of your planning committee agree on a strategy, and the tenth is willing to implement it only over his dead body? What is the best course of action when the group is evenly divided on an issue? What if two mutually exclusive options emerge, and neither seems clearly superior to the other? These questions may become very real as you deal with some of the fundamental issues facing your organization. As you examine your options for dealing with lack of consensus, all have drawbacks. Majority rules can give undue power to the best politicians or the biggest alliances. Flipping a coin can seem to be an attractive management tool at times, but is probably not the best way to charge ahead and create a future. Having the chairperson of the committee decide and issue the recommendation may invite mutiny.

Words such as compromise, understanding, authority, and responsibility must find their way into a discussion of these issues. Perhaps with several minor modifications to a plan, all involved could support it. Maybe the heart of the issue is a misperception of the implications of a particular course of action, and the particulars need to be spelled out carefully, one more time. In the final analysis, it is up to the top administrators, the chief executive officer, and the board of directors to make decisions. If, after reasonable exploration, a committee or project team is unable to come to a consensus on a decision, perhaps they could spell out the opposing viewpoints or offer a majority and minority report for the next level up to review.

Consensus on important issues is an ideal state of affairs, and should be sought whenever possible. Reaching a consensus on the plan will help enlist the support and action needed to carry out the organization's plans. If consensus is not possible, extra effort may be needed to pull the dissenters into the process of implementing plans they opposed. However, in any business, employees are paid to further the goals of the corporation and not their own. It is normal and healthy for staff turnover to occur at times of change, when existing personnel become dissatisfied with the course of events and new staff members are happy to become a part of the new guard. While not always easy, the needs of the organization must come first.

Getting Bogged Down

Working on the development of a strategic plan can be difficult, time-consuming, and even discouraging, especially if some of the problems and pitfalls described above sound familiar. There are so many things to consider, and important decisions to be made. Then there are the day-to-day crises and operations to attend to. In the midst of all this, it is easy to become bogged down.

Bogging down can be a symptom of trying to do too much, working with difficult people, or simple burnout. Step back and look at what you've done and exactly where you are stuck. Maybe you need to discuss a problem with an outsider, or process an issue further with staff. Perhaps you need to realize that planning is never done and that you will not nail down the best way to do everything forever. Maybe you need a vacation. Try to discover and treat the cause of whatever's bogging you. Remember that strategic planning is simply a mechanism to answer questions about your organization's future and develop a better tomorrow. It deserves your best effort, and you'll need to keep moving toward your goals one step at a time.

5

Marketing Your Organization

If a tree falls in the forest and there's no one there to hear, does it make a noise?

George Berkeley

If your organization is terrific, wonderful and stupendous, and nobody knows about you or utilizes what you have to offer, how effective are you at doing what you do? This fundamental question forms the basis for the necessity of nonprofit marketing.

Marketing is sometimes still thought of as a dirty word in nonprofit circles. It can conjure up images of snake oil salesmen and medicine men making extravagant claims about the value of their product to humanity, while their true motivation was simply to make a buck. While no one will argue with the merits of making a buck, the pursuit of profit is not the reason nonprofit organizations exist. Marketing can take on a new meaning when applied to nonprofit organizations.

FOR-PROFIT VERSUS NONPROFIT MARKETING

There are both similarities and differences in marketing concepts and techniques in for-profit and nonprofit organizations. In each case, the role of marketing is determining the needs of the consuming public, providing input on filling that need, and then making the public aware of the product or service that will fill the identified need. Whether the need is toothpaste or education, the process of marketing planning is somewhat similar.

One important difference between for-profit and nonprofit marketing can be the role and philosophy of creating a demand. While a toy company would love to see one of their dolls in every household in the country, a social service agency would hardly look forward to the day that every family would become consumers of their services for disabled children. Since much of the nonprofit world is devoted to dealing with the problems of humanity, it is not appropriate in many cases to think of creating a market for one's services. Otherwise, breweries and alcoholism programs would team up to promote the consumption of more beer in order to increase their markets. A similarity does exist, however, in that nonprofits should have a goal of reaching those in need; providing access to and information about services is one of the valid functions of nonprofit marketing.

While for-profit and nonprofit enterprises may have different bottom-line goals, marketing is geared to helping both reach those goals. Making money may be the objective of major corporations, and reaching those in need of services to improve their lives in some way may be the goal of nonprofits, but marketing plays an important role either way. Whether your goal is serving the financial needs of your stockholders or the intangible needs of your stakeholders, a solid marketing plan will help you along your way.

Money, however, cannot be discounted as an important factor in nonprofit management. Without sufficient funds to operate, you will be unable to benefit anyone. It is perfectly legitimate for a nonprofit organization to see its marketing function as a means to increase revenue over expenses in order to improve its capacity to operate and grow. This is not in conflict with the principles or the concept of nonprofit organizations. Your services ultimately are not free; the funds come from somewhere and allow you to be successful in carrying forth your mission.

Competition is also a very real phenomenon in nonprofit management. Hospitals are keenly aware of this fact, as are many other agencies vying for limited funds. If your area can no longer support two small colleges in the same fashion as in the past and one is likely to close, wouldn't it be nice if it were the other one? This is not to say that you wish your colleagues badly, but at times the concept of survival of the fittest applies to nonprofit businesses as well. Grants, student applications, client enrollment in your programs, and support of your cause are all issues where competition comes into play. A solid marketing plan can help you to come out on top.

Competition in the nonprofit arena can take on a different quality; while a consumer may choose a videocassette recorder on the basis of cost, nonprice competition is a frequent phenomenon in nonprofits. If a hospital stay is covered by insurance, the consumer will not be particularly concerned over his or her admission to more expensive Hospital

A over Hospital B ten minutes away with lower charges. Services on a sliding scale or that are offered free will not encourage much interest in competitive pricing issues. Many times it is other issues, such as reputation, proximity, and visibility, that will make the difference in nonprofit marketing; the service must appeal to the sensibilities rather than the pocketbook.

In any type of marketing, packaging and visibility are important factors. Just as the manufacturers of laundry detergent and breakfast cereal continually update and brighten their packages to "grab" the consumer, the nonprofit marketer must be sure that the service and programs of the organization are attractive and appealing to the potential consumer. Research has shown that different marketing approaches appeal to various socioeconomic groups, and this is also a factor for nonprofits. An agency attempting to attract wealthy "paying customers" might have packaging problems associated with a location in the wrong part of town. However, a casual storefront approach might prove most effective with other segments of the population. Attractive brochures, colorful posters, and dynamic speakers are just a few of the ways nonprofit organizations can attractively package their services to attract potential customers.

Quality can never be underestimated as a marketing tool. Just as a person who has had a delicious meal at a restaurant can be a valuable member of its marketing staff, a mother whose dyslexic child has been helped or a patron who has enjoyed the new display at the museum will become assets in spreading the news of the organization. In nonprofit agencies, the line between public relations and marketing blurs; if people know about you, hear positive things about you, and feel you can serve their needs, you are successfully marketing your organization.

Marketing can take many forms. Some organizations might have such a tight referral network or positive word of mouth that they need not feel much concern over creating a demand for their services. Others may have serious utilization problems or hot competitors, and for them marketing takes on a greater urgency. In either case, it is beneficial to learn more about the people in your market; discover who they are, what they want and need, and what attracts them. The development of a solid marketing plan can help you to grow, or can simply help you to maintain the status quo if that is your goal. It is difficult to imagine developing a strategy for the future without taking into consideration the needs and preferences of those who consume your services, and identifying those whose needs remain unmet, so that you can move into new markets if that is your interest.

MARKETING VERSUS SELLING

There is a very real difference between developing a marketing orientation in your organization and becoming sales oriented. Marketing is an activity that should be the precursor to all you do, and a step ahead of selling.

• Marketing is a consumer-based activity designed to allow you to identify actual and potential customers; assess their needs, attitudes, and preferences; and address your plans to the realities determined by the investigation of your market. It is aimed at filling the needs of consumers by offering them programs or services they will find attractive, beneficial, or useful.
• Selling is an organization-based activity aimed at motivating others to consume what your organization has to offer. It is geared toward filling the needs of the organization by selling its programs and services in order to ensure its survival and profitability.

Ideally, as you develop your strategic plan you will develop a marketing orientation; this ingredient belongs at the front end of your planning, while sales strategies can be developed as the plan unfolds.

Like the old story about selling refrigerators to Eskimos, very few of us would relish the idea of providing services to black teen-agers in an all-white community or opening a child-care center to serve a retirement home. Perhaps a dynamite sales force could drum up some business by offering transportation to the site or developing a convincing sales pitch. None of these sales strategies, however, can be effective if the marketing planning was faulty or overlooked a few basic facts. Before you decide to set up a program or embark on a new strategy, some marketing-oriented thinking is in order.

You will probably find that your plans are more successful if they are developed with the needs of the consuming public in mind. Looking at such factors as population demographics, geographic location, and the presence and activities of competitors are all marketing-oriented actions that can help you to create a favorable future. By investigating whether a market exists for specific services, you can work toward developing an organization that is in tune with the times.

Looking at the potential market for your services can include a number of factors:

• Do people need what we plan to offer? A program for the elderly in an area with the lowest median age in the county may be doomed to failure.
• Are people willing to utilize what we have to offer? A mental health facility in an ethnic community that values keeping problems in the family and under wraps may face some problems; while the "need" may exist, if the community is unwilling to admit to that need, you will be fighting an uphill battle.
• Who else is offering a similar service? An area crowded with competitors will probably have little need for your services, and poor utilization could result.
• Who are our potential customers? Knowing to whom you will be offering your services will help you to develop a strategy that will offer maximum appeal to that target population.

The list of marketing factors for your organization could be lengthy, and should reflect the realities within which you operate. As you think about your market, sales strategies will also probably emerge; an important part of marketing is carrying the word of your existence to those you have identified as being in need of your services. Both marketing and sales play an important role in the success of an organization, but realizing that marketing is a vital component of planning will help you to develop sound strategies.

UNDERSTANDING THE NEED FOR MARKETING IN NONPROFIT ORGANIZATIONS

There are a number of business reasons for marketing nonprofit organizations, and a number of humanitarian reasons as well. A well-run business allows you to be more effective in providing services and programs to your target populations.

No one would argue that nonprofits have long done excellent work in increasing public awareness of problems, needs, and solutions. Campaigns to increase adult literacy, prevent child abuse, find missing children, and detect cancer in its early stages can be cited as examples of ways that nonprofit organizations have made a significant public impact. Yet these can be considered effective marketing tools as well. Good marketing and public relations activities will not only benefit the organization, they will benefit the public. Every time an individual seeks services to help a disabled child, donates money to medical research, or calls a hotline rather than striking a child, nonprofit marketing has benefited both the organization whose business has just grown and the public it seeks to serve. It is also a possible outcome that your advertising or publicity will lead potential consumers to seek a similar service elsewhere; perhaps you have made marital counseling sound so worthwhile that a couple will seek it at an agency nearer home. This outcome is also desirable; any activity that generates interest in your field will ultimately benefit you, and will indirectly benefit countless others.

Letting people know that you're there allows them to make informed choices on their options. Not everyone will be interested in your organization, but the information you provide will likely contribute to the greater good. No one will seek your services and programs in the absence of adequate information. Unless you operate by invitation only, you will need to be seen and known in order to do what you want to do. Marketing, then, is useful for fostering community awareness of problems and services and the effectiveness of the organizations that provide them.

Increasing or maintaining the utilization of your services can best be achieved through marketing activities of some type. Many nonprofits have reported increases in calls, clients, and customers following the airing of a public service announcement or the appearance of a feature article on their services in the local newspaper. Obviously, favorable utilization is needed for all you do. Whether you are fee for service, publicly funded, or receive grant money from private foundations, your future depends on people knowing about and using your services.

Marketing, if done ethically and humanely, is not a crass and exploitative activity for nonprofit organizations. It is a means of fostering the interaction between organization and consumer, information-giver and information-seeker in a way that is beneficial to both. Marketing can be a vital part of your organization's future success.

DEVELOPING A MARKETING ORIENTATION

The first step toward developing a marketing orientation is to build it into your programs and services. At times, conflict can emerge between the needs of those who provide services and those who are concerned with their success in the marketplace. This need not happen if you see the two as integral pieces of the same whole.

In looking at new and existing services, it is beneficial to keep an eye on the market. Build in goals for the utilization of your services, and investigate shortfalls. Look at who is using your service and whether they differ from the target population you had in mind at the project's inception. Examine how you are promoting your organization, to whom, and whether your promotional efforts are proving effective in arousing interest in your existence. By integrating these activities into your operations, you begin to develop a marketing orientation that is not separate from or in conflict with your program efforts.

Take a look at your mission, and apply marketing concepts within that framework. If your mission statement relates to the provision of post-secondary education to liberal-arts majors, what are you doing to further that mission? You will be unable to provide the education if you do not first find potential students and interest them in your curriculum. Marketing is probably implied in your mission; few nonprofit organizations would develop a mission statement that relates, "XYZ Agency exists to sell counseling services to victims of physical abuse," but your effectiveness in serving those victims will depend on your ability to reach them and facilitate their entry into your service system. Chances are that marketing activities in some form play a key role in your ability to carry forth your stated mission.

You can also become a more effective service provider if you develop a true marketing orientation. By keeping in touch with the needs of your consumers, you can better fill those needs. Knowing that the population in your area is changing or that social realities have altered the way of life of your constituency can help you gear up to meet those changing needs, ensuring your survival in the process. Again, marketing is not a "separate" activity confined to your marketing or public relations staffs, if you have them. It is an integral part of organizational effectiveness.

Strategic positioning is the development of a favorable spot in the environment in which you operate, and is a useful concept in the development of organizational and marketing strategies. It takes into account many of the factors mentioned above: the population, social factors, the actions of your competitors. Examining data generated through environmental scanning can help you to determine what your position should be with regard to those issues in order to maintain a favorable position in your market.

MARKET RESEARCH, INFORMATION, AND ANALYSIS

Formal market research is a complex, time-consuming, and often expensive activity. While some nonprofit organizations have the ability to hire market research firms or develop sophisticated market research departments in-house, many do not. This does not mean that you must remain ignorant of the world around you; there are some relatively simple ways to gain marketing-related information that may prove useful if interpreted with caution.

Deciding What You Need to Know

The number of knowable facts in the universe is probably infinite, as is the amount of time needed to discover every one. Therefore, it will be to your advantage to zero in on what you really need to know. You can discover, with minimal digging, some interesting facts about your organization and the environment in which it operates. You can dig even deeper and do analyses of some of these facts in terms of other data. You can do formal research on the preferences and reactions of different segments of your clientele. How far you go depends on your needs, time, money, and expertise.

At the very least, you should identify some basic internal and external information needs. If you have already been gathering program data in an organized, systematic way, you will be ahead of the game. Also, if you have established ways of collecting information on competitors, funding, and the world and people around you, this will be a plus. In any case, review your statements of needs and interests in developing a strategic plan. Identify the major areas you have targeted, and begin to ask questions about each. Then determine what information you will need to answer each of those questions. For example, if you have decided to explore the feasibility and advisability of opening a branch campus of your educational institution, you will need to focus on key questions, which might include:

- Where do your present students live?
- What geographic areas contain a large number of people who meet the description of your target market?
- What other competing schools are in the area and what are their approximate market shares?
- Has enrollment in your present institution been declining or growing over the past five years?
- What areas appear to be underserved by similar schools and therefore might be good targets for your program?

Identifying questions such as these will allow you to zero in on important market-oriented areas. You will then know what data to gather and how to proceed in your analysis of that data. Finding the answers to the above questions will provide you with an important set of facts to use in proceeding with your planning. Asking well-defined, answerable questions will keep you from wasting time in digging out useless facts and will help you to focus your efforts.

Identifying Your Market

Knowing who you serve is an essential part of understanding your present situation and planning for the future. You can learn a great deal about your present clientele by asking some basic questions that you may be able to answer by examining your organization's records. The questions naturally will vary from organization to organization, but might include variables such as:

- Place of residence
- Age
- Income
- How they first became aware of your organization
- Marital status
- Educational level
- Occupation
- Number of children
- Previous experiences with similar organizations
- Whether they were referred to you by a third party
- Type of service rendered by your organization to each consumer
- Length of involvement with your organization

Selecting and analyzing variables such as those listed above will allow you to answer some important and interesting questions about your market. Suppose you discover that your market at a community mental health center consists primarily of 45–year-old housewives that have teen-aged children and live in the community in which you are based. You have gathered some information that might have important implications for marketing, such as:

- Women's groups might be a good service for you to offer.
- Workshops on dealing with teen-agers might be well utilized.
- You might want to consider opening an outreach center in a nearby town, since that area is not currently being served by your center.
- Additional informational efforts might be needed to publicize your children's services.
- You might consider strategies to help men feel more comfortable in seeking your services.

By examining information about your existing clientele, you can determine both who your market is and who it is not. You can then choose to increase your services to those you are already in contact with, appeal to those you are not currently reaching, or some combination of the two. If you are unaware of who your market is, however, you will be prone to shooting in the dark and may move in a perfectly appealing direction with one major flaw—there is no market for what you are doing!

Another aspect of market identification is the targeting of additional groups. Suppose you discover that residents of a neighboring town have the highest per capita income in the county and you are interested in developing a wellness and fitness program for paying customers. The residents of this town might make a good target for brochures, posters, and talks to local organizations about the benefits of your program. Determining your optimal target population will help you to design programs and market your efforts. You might find it helpful to visualize your "ideal" client; if you want to market your wellness program to women aged 35 to 45 who are free in the mornings and have family incomes that exceed $25,000, you have successfully defined your target, and now can determine where such people reside and how they might be interested in your services.

Trends and Patterns

Looking at facts in isolation and out of context can lead to some fairly wild conclusions. Determining that all of the women on your caseload who developed breast cancer live in the same town may not be surprising if 95 percent of your clients live in that town. Discovering that your fee-for-service weight loss counseling program lost money after five successful years of operation should not shock you if the local mill closed and half the residents of your area are struggling to survive. One fact often makes little sense unless it is examined as part of larger trends and patterns.

Historical data is very important in the strategic planning process. Being able to look at your performance over time can give useful clues to areas that warrant further examination or action. It will also allow you to form hypotheses to explain these changes and trends, and help you to predict or control the future. Trends and patterns form the basis of much of scientific inquiry, and can provide a solid basis from which to exercise the art of decision-making. Rather than generalizing from a single case or a few observations, looking at the "big picture" over time will allow you to make more accurate observations. Computerized information systems are ideal tools to assist you in this endeavor; it is possible to quickly and easily summarize several years' data in key areas.

Both internal and external data can and should be examined for trends and patterns. Discovering that more males than females have used the services of your organization each year can provide interesting input into your planning process. A steadily growing number of elderly residents in your community can mean new opportunities or necessitate changes in your services and programs. By closely examining trends, you can also begin to predict the future without the use of a crystal ball. If the population in your county has grown over each of the last ten years, it may be quite likely that it will increase again next year, and you can factor that into your plans. Naturally, you need to look out for floods, earthquakes, and plant closings, which could cause a mass exodus from the area. The future is never completely predictable, but examining available data allows us to make predictions as accurately and scientifically as possible.

Questionnaires and Interviews

Some of the data you seek may not be readily available in your archives or the records of demographers. You may want to know other, more subjective, or specialized information relevant to your organization. Often the best way to get it is to ask.

Planning proceeds most smoothly when you have a solid handle on the needs, preferences, and reactions of consumers and potential consumers. Perhaps you need to know how they feel about a specific aspect of your services or how you might better serve their needs in some area. Information such as this might best be gathered by questionnaires or interviews.

Naturally, the investigation of attitudes is significantly less scientific than the examination of the number of males and females you contacted last year. People may not be clear on their own feelings, they may be reluctant to express themselves honestly, or may choose not to respond at all. For these reasons, the use of questionnaires and interviews can only approximate reality to some extent. However, they may in many cases be the best tools available for measuring the imprecise realities of human nature. A careful mapping out of what you want to know and how you will determine it will ensure the best possible results.

Suppose you want to determine your clients' reasons for choosing your services over those of another agency. This may be a worthwhile question to ask, as it will help you to determine critical factors in your success and measure your effectiveness in reaching the public. How you ask the question can make a big difference in the objectivity and usefulness of the responses. There are also several ways to gather the information you seek.

• Questionnaires can be used to determine answers to such questions. They may include open-ended questions, such as, "How did you first hear about our organization?" and forced choice questions, such as, "How important was our location as a factor in your choice to come to this agency?" accompanied by a five-point scale. A real advantage to questionnaires is that they are simple to administer, and can be more objective, as each person surveyed is asked the same questions in the same way. A person might also be more honest when responding to a piece of paper than a live human who might be offended by the answer.
• Interviews can be more time-consuming and cumbersome, but can provide qualitative information that might not be determined by a questionnaire. By talking with the interviewee directly, it is possible to pick up nuances and shades of meaning that might not be detected on a questionnaire. People may also be more cooperative and less likely to respond to the personal approach that interviews provide. However, interviews also run the risk of being less precise. Questions may be asked somewhat differently by each interviewer, and the interviewee's responses may be colored by the characteristics of the interviewer. Imagine a nun conducting interviews on attitudes toward birth control and abortion, or a black interviewer asking whites about their racial prejudices. These biases can be built into interviews and greatly distort results.

How questions are asked also can affect the responses that will be given. A good rule of thumb is to be as specific, neutral, and concrete as possible. For example:

• "We have made every effort to keep our fees affordable. Do you have any comments on our fee structure?" communicates to the respondent the desired answer. It is obvious that the question is asking for a compliment; it is biased in favor of the organization.
• "Please rate our fee structure by choosing one of the following: fees are much too high, fees are slightly high, fees are affordable," is more objective and

gives the respondent more choice. You might also give the option of saying that your fees are too low, but it is unlikely that anyone will choose it!

• "Please rate our staff in terms of competence, caring, and efficiency" is a question that could have respondents in quite a quandary. Suppose your staff is competent but rude, or very nice but poorly trained, or efficient but cold and incompetent. Such a question, by trying to do too much, does too little.

• "Please rate the courtesy of our staff" is a nice, simple question that is answerable by most respondents. It deals with one dimension and can be easily quantified by a rating scale.

Open-ended questions can be very useful if asked properly and summarized and interpreted with care. Since your clients will differ in their ability to express themselves clearly, there may be times when it is difficult to determine what is actually being said, especially in written questionnaires. However, it is through open-ended questions that you can gather potentially "juicy" information you may not have thought to ask for, or anecdotal information that can help to explain attitudes and feelings toward your organization.

Forced-choice questions have ease of analysis as a major strength. You simply tally all the responses and can determine numbers and percentages of respondents who chose each option. In this clean analysis, however, you lose some important information. If someone rates your services poorly, forced-choice questions will be unable to tell you why. However, they can help you to determine problem areas and strengths for further investigation. Probably a combination of both types of questions will yield the most accurate, thorough examination of the matter you wish to investigate.

If you have decided to use interviews or questionnaires, try to get as much input as possible from a variety of sources. You probably know exactly what you mean by each question, but the meaning may not be as clear to another reader. Pilot-testing the instrument a few times may help you to work out the bugs before you go to the expense and trouble of extensive data-gathering. Remember that how you ask is a major factor in how questions will be answered.

Caution must be used in reporting on the results of questionnaires and interviews. We all have our own biases and viewpoints, and are likely to be happy when the results agree with our opinions and unhappy when they do not. Objectivity is essential, however. When the report is discussed is the appropriate time to offer personal observations and opinions, not in the preparation of the report. Stick to the facts—only the facts.

Client or Customer Satisfaction Surveys

Satisfaction surveys are a special breed of informational tool that deserves some mention. In any business, the satisfaction of your customers and/or related persons will play an important factor in your success. While a survey of patients in a chronic psychiatric ward of a state hospital or children in an immunization clinic may not yield useful results, surveying consumers (or, if appropriate, their relatives) might help you to gather information that can help you to identify areas that are perceived as particular strengths or weaknesses.

Some businesses, such as hospitals, might do satisfaction surveys on a regular basis, contacting a certain sample of their patients and compiling the results in a profile that is useful for both marketing and program evaluation. Others may only ask when there is a particular question that appears to warrant investigation. The use of such surveys can help you to determine consumer preferences and reactions, and can help you to understand their attitudes and behavior toward your organization. This type of tool can help identify why clients drop out of programs, why they continue to utilize your programs and services, and how you can serve them better. It may be worthwhile to consider periodic surveys of your clientele or segments of your market in order to stay in touch with their very real perceptions of who you are and how you're doing.

Personal Follow-Up

If you are committed to the satisfaction of your clientele or stakeholders, you may want to consider looking at responses individually as well as in summary form. By examining individual responses, you can pinpoint specific problems and areas of discontent. In those cases, it may be worth your while to follow-up the response with a personal contact. Such personal contact can accomplish several tasks:

• You can gather more in-depth information on the reasons behind the response. If a client gave a low rating to the courtesy of your staff, why did that occur? Discovering that your receptionist swore at a consumer of your services is important in doing some short-range planning with the receptionist. That the client felt he was treated more professionally at another agency can be useful information.

• You can take advantage of a valuable public relations opportunity. By making a personal contact on a complaint or comment, you are communicating very clearly that you do care and are eager to become aware of and deal with problems. This approach can help you to be more in touch with the feelings of your constituency while bringing them firmly into your corner.

• Your staff can be involved in dealing with the public in a meaningful way. By dividing the workload into small packages, a number of persons can share the responsibility for making personal contacts. They can learn a valuable lesson on the importance of public relations in the process.

Some Cautions

Information gleaned from interviews, surveys, or other means of informal research should not be taken as law. Unless you have gone to great pains to select your sample randomly, gather information scientifically, and provide controls and sophisticated analyses, your data is probably open to question and should not be seen as conclusive. However, such information can prove useful if several cautions are kept in mind.

Any time a small sample is used to make generalizations about a larger population, there is the possibility of error. If you ask the next three people who walk into your reception area how they feel about your services and they all give you an identical answer, it is tempting to conclude that their perception is the opinion others will hold as well. However, there could be many other factors operating. You could interview the next three and get an entirely different answer—perhaps the first responses were merely coincidences. Also, those three respondents could have special characteristics. Perhaps they were all members of a therapy group geared to depressives; that certainly would color their perspective. If you are dealing with small samples, be cautious in your interpretation. It might serve you well to see the information gleaned as "clues" that will guide you in further investigation of a potentially important issue.

You also need to keep in mind the characteristics of the respondents. Surveying the satisfaction of court-ordered offenders will be likely to produce far more negative results than interviewing a group of suburban women who are voluntarily attending a fitness program. Some groups may not be reliable informants, or their perceptions may be clouded by the very problems that brought them to your organization if you are geared to human services.

In any case, information gathered through any form of informal "research" can be only as good as the persons interpreting it. By placing it within the framework of what you already know about your organization, you can begin to piece together the "big picture." Jumping to conclusions without some thoughtful analysis can yield a chaotic situation where inappropriate action is taken on inconclusive evidence.

IDENTIFYING COMPETITORS

Knowing who your competitors are and what they are doing is a key ingredient to your market analysis. Since an important factor in strategic planning is developing strategies for survival and growth, you will need to become aware of others in your environment who might be threats or impediments to your goals.

Defining your competitors is the first step; it takes a thorough analysis of those around you and their actual and potential impact. It may be easy to identify some of your major competitors, but others may be less obvious. For example, a community hospital's major competitors may be two other hospitals located within a ten-mile radius. Their services are similar and their status as competitors is obvious. Think, however, of the other options potential patients might seek when in need of medical services: urgent-care centers, private clinics, larger hospitals in nearby cities, or regional centers specializing in specific illnesses. If the hospital had the ability to track every potential patient, it would be able to determine that it loses a certain number to each of these facilities.

A zoo might also find itself in a position of competing against unlikely competitors. Other zoos in the area might be obvious competitors, but the symphony, library, museum, and planetarium might also compete for that segment of the market seeking educational or cultural activities. The amusement park, a sports event, and miniature golf might compete for the group seeking a pleasant family outing on a Sunday afternoon. If it were possible to interview each person who considered going to the zoo during a given week, you would be able to determine that a number of competing activities triumphed, and that a significant number of people probably decided to stay home and relax. Therefore, in looking at marketing issues, the goal here is to convince the public that the zoo is more attractive than other activities, including relaxation.

Be as creative as possible in defining your competitors, and try to develop an initial list that includes a number of possibilities. The question you are trying to answer is, "What other choices are available to people who are potential consumers of our services and programs?" By answering this question, you can begin developing strategies to place your organization in a more attractive position than those identified as competitors.

Competitive Analysis

Once you have identified your competitors, you can begin to develop an understanding of the position of each relative to your organization. This analysis can take several forms.

First, gather as much data as you can on your significant competitors. Find out what they're doing, how they're doing, and what they're likely to do in the future. To some extent, this information can be gathered without late-night break-ins and the deployment of troops and spies. The organization's annual report and program brochures will be good sources of information. There may also be an informal information network where buzzings about other organizations can be heard. Chances are that someone on your staff knows something about your competitors via a friend or relative. Sometimes published data will be available; this may be the case in areas such as health care and publicly funded programs. By exploring a number of potential sources of information and making a concerted effort to compile what you know, you can develop a fairly good understanding of your competitors and the part they play in the overall environment.

After some preliminary data has been collected, a scaled-down version of the SWOT analysis can be used to examine each significant competitor. Look at their strengths, weaknesses, opportunities, and threats. Use all the information you have available to make educated guesses about the position of competing organizations. By identifying their strengths and weaknesses, you will gain additional information concerning your own opportunities and threats. A strong program of a competitor may spell trouble or indicate a need for change in your competing programs, whereas a weak program may identify an opportunity for your growth and expansion in that area. By carrying out a detailed analysis, you may also be able to anticipate your competitors' moves to some extent. You may be able to piece together their overall directions and plans so that you can either hasten your entry into the market or concede a certain program to them and concentrate your efforts in other, unique areas.

Estimation of Market Shares

In the absence of complete disclosure of data in many areas, it is probably difficult to impossible to determine precisely what percentage of consumers choose your services or those of your competitors. If you knew that exactly 100 people sought physical therapy in your town last month (25 at Hospital A, 30 at Clinic B, 40 at Hospital C, and 5 at your facility) you would be in possession of certain key facts about the market:

- No one facility currently holds a monopoly on the market for physical therapy services.
- Hospital C was successful in attracting the largest share (40 percent of the market).
- You have some serious work to do.

However, in the absence of such explicit data, you can still make some estimates based on the information you have available. From sources of revenue on annual reports, you may be able to determine how well utilized your competitors' services have been. Published data may yield some figures on the position of each competitor in the marketplace. Your goal here is to get a general idea of the power of each of your competitors in drawing in potential consumers. There are a number of potential methods for measuring the concept of market share. It is possible to use figures regarding the amount of revenue pulled down by each competitor for similar services, and determine the percentage of income for those services received by each of a well-defined pool of competitors. In some agencies, looking at the number of clients or the number of visits and calculating the percentage captured by each competitor may make sense. You will be limited by the amount and type of information publicly available and that you can gather from your competitors through conversation, publications, or annual reports. Unless you are certain that a complete disclosure has been made by each of the organizations you are studying, your data will be incomplete; it will represent a ball-park figure and should be treated as such—as a guide for further study and not a definitive indication of your standing in the marketplace.

Knowing where you stand relative to others can give you crucial information for your planning process. It can help you to understand the market in which you operate, and can help you to identify your primary competitors. This analysis can also help you to get a handle on the successes of others, and how you stack up against them.

Prioritizing and Targeting Competitors

This may not be war, where you determine the enemy's position in an effort to blow him out of the water, but it does help to know who to watch and how to strengthen your own position relative to others. After you have completed your analysis of the strengths, weaknesses, and approximate market shares of your competitors, you can begin placing them in priority order. How you do this must be left to your own judgment based on the importance of various factors in your situation. For example, the competitor with the largest market share may not be number 1 on your list if a new competitor is growing fast and has designs on your market and clientele. A dissimilar organization may be your biggest competitor; perhaps a hypnosis center has just opened in your community, promising quick, painless results against smoking, over-eating, anxiety, and depression and is draining clients from your psychological services.

Using whatever criteria are meaningful for you, try to arrange your competitors in priority order. Then reexamine the characteristics of each in an effort to determine what strategies might be useful against them. Looking at the programs, strengths, and weaknesses of your chief competitors in some detail may give you a significant advantage in engineering your own survival and growth.

Cooperation versus Competition

There may be times when it makes sense to work cooperatively rather than competitively with other organizations. This can be done in a number of ways:

• You may choose to work jointly with another organization on a project, combining your expertise and splitting the revenue and expense. A program for the overstressed parents of disabled children might be the result of a joint project between a parental stress center and an organization serving disabled children.

• You may choose to concede a particular market to another organization. For example, in an area with little demand for geriatric day care, such services might best be left to one provider rather than attempting to divide a small market to no one's benefit.

• You can develop referral networks for working cooperatively on a number of issues. By recognizing the areas of expertise of other agencies, you can refer your clients to those organizations for their programs and services that complement rather than compete with yours, and encourage referrals to your organization in the process.

• You can agree to "divide" services in some way—you handle Program A, and we'll do Program B to avoid duplication of services and competition in some areas.

The pros and cons of each of these options will need to be explored in some depth according to the needs, goals, and realities of your organization. An important factor in a competitive versus cooperative decision is the position and character of the other organization. Is it basically a "friend" with whom a comfortable relationship has existed over time, or does it have a reputation as a real barracuda? Is the area in question one you will later regret not having developed by yourself, or is the market for the service fairly stable? Will you be helping the organization to compete with you in other areas if you work cooperatively on one venture? These and other issues deserve thorough exploration before you decide what your position regarding competitors will be.

The real advantage to joint ventures is that both parties share the risk and expenses, and may be able to enter markets together that either would have been unable to reach alone. Be aware, though, that revenue and glory will also be shared if the venture is successful, and that your control over the project will be limited to some extent by the wishes of your partner. Try to think through such issues and build into the agreement terms that will be beneficial to your organization. If the partnership becomes significant or formalized, you will probably need to consult an attorney to ensure that your rights and privileges are clearly spelled out, and that the partnership is in your best interests.

MARKETING TECHNIQUES

Although effective marketing techniques will vary tremendously from organization to organization, it will be to your advantage to give some thought to how you will promote your programs and services so that this promotion can be built into the plans for the programs and the strategic plan as a whole. The definition of all the details need not be completed at this stage, but since marketing issues are so crucial to strategic planning, outlining marketing considerations early in the process will probably prove beneficial.

A good question to ask yourself as you develop your plans might be, "How can we get people to use this service?" By thinking about this question as you develop new services or explore existing ones, you are integrating programs and markets—a useful habit to develop. You are probably familiar with some marketing techniques such as the following:

• *Public service announcements.* Many nonprofit agencies take advantage of these opportunities to carry their message through television and radio. These announcements can reach large audiences and help inform the public about your programs and services. They can also provide useful information on an issue with which your organization is involved, such as adult literacy, child abuse, or smoking. You can determine your "ideal client" or target market and then aim your efforts at stations that reach those segments: rock stations for teenage drug abuse, easy listening for older populations, and classical for educational or cultural programs, for example.

• *Advertising.* Nonprofit organizations that have or can raise funds for advertising can reach large audiences through wise media buying. TV, radio, newspaper, or magazine ads can also be targeted for specific markets, and can be effective in raising public awareness of your existence and services.

• *Media coverage.* Some of the best public exposure can be free if you can attract periodic attention of the news media. A feature story on your programs or an interview with a member of your staff can provide a great deal of good publicity and help you to achieve recognition as the "experts" in your field. Building a good relationship with the media can be very profitable.

• *Marketing staff.* Some nonprofits whose budgets will allow it have added staff members whose sole purpose is to familiarize the public and various segments of the market with the purpose and services of the organization. Some organizations have added public relations functions to the duties of other staff members. Whether or not your organization can afford to hire specialized marketers, you may want to consider building some promotion activities into the jobs of other members of your team.

• *Referral networks.* This type of marketing cannot be underestimated as a tool for gaining consumers for your services. A real advantage is that it is a low-cost means of developing pathways for attracting those with a need for or interest in your services. Because of good relationships with other organizations, you can be funneled a number of referrals. This type of network exists among physicians, where general practitioners serve as referral agents for specialists in a number of fields. Similarly, you can work on developing a reputation as an expert resource and let likely referral agents know of your existence.

• *Direct mail.* Once you have targeted your market audience, it is possible to contact them by mail. Although not free, direct mail can be a reasonable method of reaching potential consumers. You can buy or develop mailing lists, and can target various segments of the population by specific demographic characteristics or by geographic location. This can be an effective means of informing the public of your existence and programs, and appealing to them according to their unique characteristics.

• *Goodwill and word of mouth.* This is a very valuable source of new business for any nonprofit organization, and is worth building in any way possible. By making consumer satisfaction a priority, you can begin to build a loyal base of supporters who will continue to utilize your services and refer others to you. Making your staff aware of the importance of courtesy and efficiency and developing a positive front for the public are vitally important in promoting goodwill for your organization.

This brief overview of marketing techniques is intended to dovetail with the development of overall marketing strategies; the random or haphazard use of any one of these techniques is unlikely to benefit your organization greatly. Again, the importance of effective planning comes into play; in developing your organization into a marketable one, you can integrate appropriate strategies directed toward meeting your own well-defined goals. Obviously, mailing or advertising will not prove very beneficial if you are not clear on what you are promoting and why. Program promotion should be integrated into program activities as a means of allowing you to effectively deliver your services to the market for their benefit as well as yours.

FUND RAISING AS MARKETING

While the fund-raising needs and activities of your organization are unique and must be addressed as such, fund raising bears a number of fundamental similarities to the marketing strategies and activities mentioned above.

In order to effectively raise funds for your organization, you must follow a number of the same steps, beginning with the development of a fund-raising orientation. Begin thinking of funding issues as you plan and examine new and existing services. Ask yourself to whom your services might be attractive, and consider potential donors to all phases of your program. Keep in mind the interests and needs of the funders, and build fund-raising plans into your overall strategic plan. Clearly, to the extent your funding can be supplemented through philanthropy, you will be free to pursue your ideas with less fear of failure.

Some research and analysis may also be warranted in the area of fund raising. Analyze your own program records to determine who your donors have been in the past, and try to determine what they have in common or what interests them. Examine the external environment; who is competing with you for funds and who is likely to fund causes such as yours. Again, in the analysis of your competitors you may need to look at some unlikely sources; budgets stretched thin for charitable dollars may accommodate only a few charities, and you will need to develop strategies for ensuring that your organization is at the top of the list.

The identification of a "market" for your fund-raising campaign can proceed in a manner similar to that of the identification of the market for your services. By examining data on past donors and scrutinizing your analysis of the organization's stakeholders, you can get some clues regarding who has "bought" your fund-raising needs in the past, and who is likely to be willing to donate in the future. Again, specific appeals might be warranted for different segments of your donating "market." Those with a personal involvement in the work of your organization might respond to a type of appeal that is very different from what is effective with corporations and foundations. By trying to anticipate the needs, interests, and reactions of various segments of your potential donors, you can increase your chances of success. Far from being unethical, this approach merely acknowledges that your program has different facets and can legitimately be presented in various ways. Again, your goal is to provide a match between the specific needs of your organization and the unique interests of each donor group.

As in marketing, packaging is essential to effective fund raising. Presenting your cause attractively and convincingly is important. As you develop your strategic plan, you can begin to think about packaging issues, and identify how and to whom funding issues might best be presented. A well-written appeal letter clearly outlining the important reasons for donating and a clearly thought-out approach can be effective fund-raising tools.

An effective strategic plan both includes and supports long-range fund-raising strategies. As you proceed with the development of your plan, be sure that program development issues receive the attention they warrant. Otherwise, you may find yourself scrambling for funds, the last organization on the list of those who control the purse strings.

DEVELOPMENT OF THE MARKETING PLAN

As with any other undertaking, marketing works better when carried out in a well-planned, well thought-out manner. Without a plan for marketing your services, you may find yourself "shooting in the dark"; a strategy that wastes time, energy, and dollars and will not put your organization in a favorable position. A sound marketing plan will guide your organization in the initiation of new services and areas of endeavor, and will serve as your guide for selling the programs and services you have to offer.

If you have spent some time gathering and analyzing relevant data, you have the basis for your marketing plan. In order to carry out the process effectively, this data should be used as a signpost for planning. It should help you to pinpoint your present and potential markets, and serve to help you in determining what needs or markets exist that you might serve.

Starting at the Beginning

A logical starting place for the development of your marketing plan is in a careful presentation of the data. You may find that the act of summarizing or writing about your findings will bring additional insight into the marketing picture. Try to state the facts you have discovered, and draw conclusions or questions from each available piece of information. This is the time to synthesize the information you have gathered to put together the big picture on your organization's market.

Sophisticated tables and charts are not necessary, although you may find pictorial representations of your findings to be useful. Those unschooled in data analysis and lacking appreciation for numbers might be more impressed by looking at a pie chart or bar graphs than by a statement that 18 percent of your market has a particular characteristic. If your plan is to be meaningful, it is important to gear its development to your audience. If you are writing for staff whose focus is more humanitarian than quantitative, be realistic. Their training and orientation might lend itself to graphic representations more than raw data. Be sure that your staff will understand what you have to say and its implications for the organization. Unfortunately, many in our society are afflicted with the dread disease of "dataphobia." If you yourself are a sufferer, be patient and spend some time with your analysis. Eventually, if treated well, your data will speak to you, and will be on your side. Start with the simple, basic facts and think about what they might mean before looking at combinations of variables such as the percentage of single white males. By dipping in one toe at a time, your splash will seem less overwhelming.

Your marketing plan should include all the relevant information you have discovered, and indicate how this information will be used to map out your organization's future. Remember that no market equals no future, and a good market with sound plans to tap it may spell the secret of success. Identify as clearly as possible who your market currently is; describe and analyze it in any way possible. Your description might include elements such as this:

An analysis of NPO Corporation's current market suggests that we are currently serving a young population, with a mean age of 26.3. This represents a change; five years ago our average customer was 35.2 years of age, and last year 29.7. In addition, our geographic base has shifted; in the past three years, customers have increasingly come from Nexttown rather than Ourtown. Presently, only 31 percent reside in Ourtown. Our efforts last year at marketing our services in Ourtown yielded a brief but temporary rise in customers from that area; for two months, the service to those residents rose, but it then fell off to its original levels.

Although this analysis is not particularly sophisticated and does not rely on expensive software packages for its existence, it does give the organization some preliminary information as a starting point. Such an introductory section, perhaps accompanied by charts and graphs, will serve as a good entry into the development of your marketing plan. It will help the reader as well as the developer of the plan to understand the present position, and should serve to catch the interest of all involved. Often, as we are caught up in day-to-day business with our individual clients, we fail to stop and think what they are like in the aggregate. This type of analysis can help your staff to think in more global terms about the services they provide, and give them a glimpse of the overall picture.

Target Groups

Each service or component of your program should have readily identified target groups. You should become so familiar with the members of these groups that you can almost recognize them on the street. Know who you exist to serve, and to whom you plan to sell your services. Your target groups should be as clearly defined as possible. If you have already taken a look at some basic strategy issues, you may be in a good position to define your target groups. This may be stated very simply:

- Our publishing company markets books to college and university professors in the humanities and social sciences for use as textbooks in their courses.
- We plan to provide dialysis services to all end-stage renal failure patients who are served by Peter, Paul, and Mary Hospitals.
- This program is aimed at providing supportive living arrangements in a halfway house setting for male prisoners being released from Upriver State Prison.
- We plan to market our day-care services to professional women who reside within a five-mile radius of our center and have a family income in the $35,000 to $50,000 range.

Such a statement of target market should be available for each of your services. You can zero in on the characteristics you feel are important in order to develop your organization in the direction you have outlined.

If you need more paying customers for building a financial base, or more women to fill new women's programs, or more professors at major universities to boost your prestige, these characteristics will help you to define your target market. If you are not sure which of several groups you will primarily serve, state your goals broadly in the beginning; that will be a start. As you further hone and develop your plans, however, try to zero in on your target market. Flexibility is in order here—although you target one group, you may find that you tend to attract another. By watching trends over time, you may need to make some revisions in your target. If your day-care services are extremely popular among those with a family income of $70,000 to $100,000, you won't want to turn them away. Your task will be to examine the implications of this data in terms of your program as a whole, and possibly to revise your marketing strategy to keep up with the realities of the changing world around you.

Marketing Goals

It is not enough to say that you want people to use your service and programs. Setting goals based on the information available and reasonable performance expectations can help you to push for success and evaluate your efforts. Is it good or bad to increase utilization by 10 percent? You may be delighted if your goal was to maintain the status quo in difficult times, or devastated if you counted on a 50 percent increase to provide the funds to subsidize a new service. Likewise, if your clients are increasingly unemployed, that may be good news if your goal was to serve the jobless. The news may be very bad if you need more paying customers to compensate for the free service you offer to others. By developing marketing goals, you provide the organization with a framework for carrying out and evaluating marketing activities.

Your goals should be based on the information you have gathered. When you look at your target population and the identification of your present clientele, this in itself may suggest a marketing goal. If you have targeted children aged five to ten years for a program and you are almost exclusively attracting children under eight, you may have an obvious marketing goal of increasing the number of children between the ages of eight and ten that you serve, or you may want to redefine the service you offer and tailor it more to the needs of the group who comprise your present market.

Marketing goals should also be related to the demographics of the people around you that you may not currently be reaching. If you have done some investigation into variables such as the population, income, types of occupation, and age in local areas, this should be helpful in setting marketing goals. For example, if your publishing company is interested in reaching more college professors with a strong interest in American history, data you have gathered on where such professors can be located and how many of them there are may help you to know if planning to increase your sales to this group by 25 percent over the next year is realistic. If there are relatively few professors of such a description and you are already reaching 85 percent of them, you may need a very brilliant strategy to reach your goal. On the other hand, if you are only reaching 10 percent of a very large pool of potential customers, a 25 percent increase may be a realistic goal indeed if you increase your marketing efforts. Only a careful examination and analysis of the data will tell you how to set your goals.

Marketing goals should encompass a number of areas, and address questions such as:

- Who are we targeting for our services and programs?
- Where might members of our target groups be located?
- How might these people best be reached?
- Who are our competitors in important target areas?
- How can we best compete in these areas?
- Is demand rising or dwindling for our service in areas we have served in the past?

When you examine such issues, you are working toward setting marketing goals based on the findings. Remember that like all goals, your marketing goals should be specific, concrete, and state exactly what you want to accomplish. When you write your marketing plan based on the information you have gathered in your analysis, anyone coming into your organization should be able to read your marketing plan and know exactly what you plan to do, and when and how you plan to do it. Otherwise, you are simply making a wish list—perhaps a good place to start, but a very vague approach to organizational planning. Since the area of marketing is so important, you will need to be very clear about what you intend to do so that you can be certain to do it.

Building in Evaluation Mechanisms

As you develop your marketing plan, you will need to ensure to the extent possible that you and your staff are accountable for following through with the plans you are developing. Although you may have a great deal of interest and enthusiasm for your plans now, you can easily lose track of your goals when you are in the heat of everyday battles. If you state your goals concretely and measurably as suggested above, you should be able to evaluate fairly easily your performance and progress toward the goals. Although it is important to state measurement tools for all goals, in the area of marketing it is especially important and, thankfully, rather easy. Here, we are generally talking about concrete measures rather than the messy business of evaluating whether neurotics get better in a therapy group or whether art gallery patrons appreciate the exhibits they view. Therefore, this area lends itself to objective evaluations.

As you develop your marketing plan, state how you will know whether your goals are met. Specific, well-written goals will be easy to measure:

- Our goal is to increase our customers in XYZ county by 10 percent over last year's figures. To evaluate this, we will use our customer records and compare figures.
- Over the next five years, we want to increase the number of return visits to our museum by 25 percent. To evaluate this, we will survey all visitors on ten randomly selected days each year and ask whether they have visited us before.
- We wish to increase our hotline service utilization by 200 calls in each of the next three years. We will begin keeping a log of all calls in order to establish a baseline measure and track all increases.

As you can see, the specification of an evaluation mechanism forces your staff to follow through and be certain that action is taken. It also pushes you to look at reasonable methods for measuring what you hope to achieve through your marketing efforts, and to plan ahead to track your progress. It is very good to set a goal of increasing your hotline calls, but if no one keeps track, how will you know whether you are reaching your goals? If you plan to increase your marketing efforts in the next county, they will be difficult to evaluate unless you have baseline or starting data and can watch to see how the data changes with your marketing efforts. It is impossible to know if you are accomplishing your goals unless you are perfectly clear on what your goals are and how you can measure progress toward them.

6
New Services and Old

Even good ideas must sooner or later degenerate into work.

Peter Drucker, *Management: Tasks—Responsibilities—Practices*

Suppose you come up with good ideas, even great ideas, on what your organization should be doing. You have thought of new programs and directions and have identified modifications you would like to make on your existing services. Good ideas are fun, entertaining, and exciting, but now comes the hard work of making them a reality.

NEW SERVICE DEVELOPMENT

Eventually, most organizations must face the idea of adding a new component or concept to their work. If you are determined to keep up with the times, you may find that needs have changed or that your clients or customers simply have different interests, problems, or life styles. And that may add up to a new service. For some organizations, especially those that have not experienced much change or have been very narrowly focused, this thought might be overwhelming and threatening. It may be difficult at first to conceive of big changes (or perhaps even little ones), and the sheer volume of detail can seem impossible. Take heart in the fact that someone, at some time, started your organization from scratch, which is a much larger task than you are now facing. As with any other project, breaking the development of a new service into its component parts may help you to tackle the undertaking and gain a feeling of accomplishment each step of the way. Translating abstract ideas into concrete, operationalized realities can challenge even the best of managers, but the alternative of avoiding these changes can have even more disastrous consequences.

Identifying Needs

Leadership has been defined as finding a parade and getting in front of it. While it may be possible to start your own parade as well, it is important to assess your parade potential early in the planning process and determine that a need for the proposed service does in fact exist. You will probably start this process with intuition; your idea seems good, and your staff is convinced that there is a need or market for your proposed service. Undoubtedly, you would not be pursuing the idea if it did not make sense on an intuitive level. Sometimes your staff's expertise and hunches can be valuable clues to the need for a new program—after all, they are knowledgeable and "experts" in the field. However, that very expertise can lead to bias. Experts can sometimes be purists and see a rather abstract and idealistic picture of reality. Your in-house experts may be very good at recognizing a legitimate need, but there may be a lack of interest in or market for the service. Starting with instinct may be necessary and legitimate as long as you recognize the need to move beyond them into some additional, more objective evaluations of your ideas.

Many of the concepts discussed in the marketing chapter are relevant to the planning of new services. If your marketing data suggests that a group remains unserved or that the demand for service is expanding in a particular component of your program, these pieces of information may provide valuable clues in assessing the need for new programs. As in all areas of strategic planning, it is important to be certain that your course of action flows with the mission and purpose of the organization. Your marketing data and plans should relate to the development of new ventures.

You may want to undertake a rather extensive investigation of market conditions before investing in a new program or service. Examination of the data you have at your disposal is a starting point. You may also want to talk with those who are knowledgeable about the area of concern, and attempt to tap their opinions and expertise. Your local library may be a good source of reading material about programs similar to the one you are interested in, and may provide useful information on how they have fared elsewhere. You can take advantage of the experience of others by visiting a similar organization that already offers the program, and doing a little brain-picking. You may need to choose carefully, and attempt to find an organization that due to geography, market, or other factors will not be a direct competitor, although you may find some competitors who are surprisingly hospitable.

Again, the subject of market research arises. It may be to your advantage to undertake a formal research project or hire skilled researchers if your undertaking is likely to be costly or involve substantial risk. You might also want to survey your stakeholders, or present or potential consumers to determine their opinions or reactions to the idea at hand. Again, this type of informal research should not be seen as conclusive in the absence of scientific techniques such as sample selection and data analysis. However, you can gain some good ideas and begin to get a grasp on how your new program or service might be received by doing some exploratory studies.

It can be difficult to set aside your enthusiasm for an idea in order to objectively evaluate its merits. It is tempting to grab onto a good idea and run with it. Testing the waters, however, is a vital first step to any new undertaking. Talk your ideas over freely with your staff and others in the field whom you trust, and evaluate the available evidence. Remember that there is no such thing as a risk-free venture; failure may impact badly on your organization in terms of finances, reputation, morale, and future directions. Therefore, it is imperative to adequately explore whether a need and market exist and whether they can be tapped in order to provide your new program with a secure future.

Criteria for New Ventures

In order to know what type of service or program will be helpful to your organization, it may be helpful to give some thought to criteria for evaluating new ventures. The definition of a "good" venture will vary greatly from one organization to the next, and will depend on the organization's unique situation in terms of finances, staffing, market, and many other factors. It would do us little good to go looking for an elephant if we did not know what elephants look like. Similarly, will we know a favorable new project when we see one?

If you have spent some time on the development of organizational goals and perhaps even a superordinate goal, it may be very simple to develop sound criteria for the evaluation of new ideas. If you have a clear idea of your organization's needs and priorities, any new program components should support and be consistent with those needs and priorities. You might think of criteria in the following terms:

• Our goal is to increase revenues in our organization as a whole. Therefore, our new programs must be projected to generate at least a 10 percent return on our investments.

86 Strategic Planning for Nonprofit Organizations

- We need to expand our reputation with physicians in this county. Our new undertakings should be geared toward making us more visible in the physician community.
- A primary goal is to attract more students into our computer science program. Therefore, we would like to develop new programs that will enhance our ability to recruit students in this area.
- We must increase the number of grants to fund our programs due to a lack of other sources of operating revenue at present. Any new projects we undertake must be in areas where grant money is available.

As you can see, what we are looking for is a symmetry between needs and realities. A perfectly valid idea just might not fit into your organization's current needs and plans. In order to avoid wasting a great deal of staff time, effort, and money, it is best to recognize your needs and what you hope to accomplish by adding new programs. If your top priority must be generating revenue, and a good idea comes along that is unlikely to be a money-maker, that is probably not the project for you.

By explicitly describing your priorities and criteria for judging ideas for new services, you can provide a structure that might be helpful in two ways.

- You have a framework for evaluating any new ideas that might arise from your strategic planning process. If you have a checklist of criteria against which to evaluate proposals, you can be assured that new ideas support your overall corporate strategy. Those that do not can quickly be discarded, giving way to more favorable proposals.
- You can use your framework as a skeleton on which to build. Once you have developed a workable set of criteria, you can devote some time and energy to developing services or programs that fit the criteria. Much like an archaeological dig, your mission is to start with a set of bones and construct a skin that will fit. Ask yourself what an animal with all your identified characteristics would look like, then set out to build one.

It will be important in the process of development of criteria to get a sense of what is vitally important and what would be nice. It is probably unusual for any new undertaking to exactly match the criteria you have developed, and therefore you must be flexible. If revenue generation is essential, then all ideas not having that characteristic might be discarded. However, if it is beneficial but not absolutely necessary to expand services into the next county, services not meeting that criterion might warrant further exploration.

A central concept in strategic planning is the development of a sound corporate identity and direction. The delineation of specific, well thought-out criteria for new areas of endeavor is one way of ensuring that you are moving in a direction that helps you to get where you want to go.

PLANNING AND THE PRODUCT LIFE CYCLE

Products and services, like people, tend to have recognizable and at times predictable life cycles. Just as we know that a baby is likely to become a child, an adolescent, an adult, a senior citizen, and eventually leave this earth, most business ventures move through similar stages. While occasionally people will die in infancy or live to be 106, it is possible to make some educated guesses about the ages at which specific developmental milestones will be reached and the life expectancy of the average man or woman born in a certain year. Likewise, by examining available information on past history and trends, it may be possible to make some ballpark predictions about the stages of any business venture.

Products, whether tangible or intangible, may be thought of as moving through four stages:

• *The birth or inception of the product.* At this point, the product is new and unknown, and often demand is low as a result. It is starting out in its infancy toward an uncertain future.
• *The growth phase of the product.* If the product is to achieve any success at all, it will grow for some period after it is introduced to the market. This growth could be a sharp rise on the graph or a gentle slope. The growth period occurs as the product receives some recognition, and demand rises as a result.
• *The leveling-off period.* Here, the big boom in growth is completed and the product enjoys a steady, predictable demand. Neither great growth nor significant loss is experienced by the product in this phase.
• *The decline of the product.* Eventually, most products begin to show downward trends on the growth charts. New products, shiny competitors, or changing times may cause the product to begin losing the attraction it once may have held.

Products may move through these cycles at vastly different rates, or may linger for long intervals in a particular stage. Products may also skip back and forth if promotion or the culture dictate. For example, the hula hoop is a product that experienced rapid growth and an equally rapid decline. Barbie dolls, however, have enjoyed some stability over a number of years. Mid-calf-length skirts have come and gone several times throughout history. You can undoubtedly chart the course of a number of products on their life cycles, and perhaps identify the factors that determined their progress through the stages.

Ideas and services move through similar stages, just as the tangible goods discussed above. Whether your organization markets health care or culture, books or birth control, it is very likely that this concept will make sense to you in evaluating both new additions and existing services. Identifying where a "product" is in its life cycle and what forces might impact on its growth and decline can help you to make informed decisions in your organizational strategy.

Most of your programs and services can probably be traced back to a starting point. Birthing rooms in hospitals, for example, were relatively unheard of a number of years ago, and you can probably identify when they were first introduced in your area. It is also possible to gather some data and watch their growth from a revolutionary new concept to a fairly common service that is used as a marketing advantage for the hospital's maternity services. Will the concept of the birthing room decline and disappear? Eventually, some new concept may replace it altogether after some period in which it is a stable offering in the health-care market. Likewise, alcoholism treatment, family therapy, types of art and home furnishings, teaching methods, and interest in issues such as child abuse and world hunger can be traced through cycles of no interest, little interest, and great interest.

Do you choose a product or service to add to your organization that is new, growing, stable, or declining? Much depends on your unique needs and your ability to take risks.

• A service in a new area could greatly add to your visibility and public image, and could be a profitable venture as well if it is successful and you are willing and able to ride out a period of low demand. Doing your homework on its prospects can help minimize your risks. Being first, innovative, and creative can add to your stature as long as your new and exciting venture doesn't fail.

• A growing area might be a good investment if you are interested in growing along with it and willing to risk being more of a follower than a leader. Depending on how fast the area is growing and how hotly your competitors are pursuing it, the growth bandwagon can be very beneficial to your organization. Be prepared, however, for the growth to top off eventually.

• A stable area might be a very safe type of venture for an organization not able or willing to take risks. If there is a piece of the market left for you, you may find stability a desirable state in terms of dependable income and clientele. While you may not be at the cutting edge of the future, you may enjoy the maturity and mainstream qualities of an investment in a stable program or service.

• A declining product is obviously one to watch out for. No one wants to be stuck with an attic full of pet rocks or a large inventory of poodle skirts. While they may come back into vogue and bring huge profits as collectors' items, they will do little to support you in the interim. If you think you have a strategy to revive waning interest or feel sure that the area is about to make a comeback, you may choose to enter the market. You may also feel that there is enough demand left to enter the market on a short-term basis with full awareness that there will come a day when you will need to pull out.

Without tarot cards and ouija boards, there may not be foolproof strategies to predict the progress of your new and existing services through their life cycles. However, past experience and an examination of the world around you may tell you what's likely to happen next. An awareness of the concept of product life cycles may help you to be aware of the fact that many of your programs might not live forever, or might require periodic fine-tuning in order to lengthen their stays in the favorable periods of growth and stability. The external realities your organization faces will also play a part in approximating the future of your ideas. A government with a poor track record on social programs, a younger or older constituency, the actions of the competition, and new breakthroughs in science and technology all might have implications for the future of your programs.

When considering a new idea, try to pin down its position relative to the concepts discussed above. Determine whether it fits into your overall corporate strategy. Are you looking for innovation? Growth? Safety? Is your new idea in a position to help you to achieve your organizational goals? Is the climate likely to favor the program's beneficial position or hasten its decline? Although you may be forced to settle for educated guesses in answer to these important questions, you will probably find yourself the better for having considered them.

EXAMINING EXISTING SERVICES

An important part of determining the soundness of your organization and its strategies is to examine your existing programs and services and how they support or detract from your organization's ability to reach its goals. Your basic programs may have been in existence for a long time, and may seem sacred. However, it is necessary to examine some of the assumptions that were quite valid a number of years ago but may be questionable at present.

If your organization has survived and is in fairly sound condition, chances are that your programs form the foundation of your success, unless your abilities in marketing have led to a triumph of style over substance. If your organization is faltering or in a state of decline, these may be symptoms of fundamental problems in your core services. Either way, what you have to offer bears periodic evaluation in order to determine whether it still provides your organization the solid base and future growth potential you desire.

Starting at the most basic point of all, it may be an interesting exercise to ask some pointed questions about your programs and services. These might include:

• Why are we doing this? The reasons you entered a particular business a number of years ago may not be valid today, or today's market may show even more need for your services. Hopefully your number 1 reason will not involve inertia or entrenchment in the status quo; if it does, you have some work to do!

• If we weren't already in this business, would we enter it today? Your answer to this question can be very revealing indeed. If there are a number of reasons that your service would not be a favorable addition under current conditions, perhaps you need to examine closely whether there exists sufficient justification to remain in that business.

• How much is this activity costing us? It is possible, especially in small organizations that lack sophisticated budgeting and reporting systems, to lose track of the cost and revenue picture on specific service components. Perhaps cost centers are not broken down in a precise way so that you can track expenses for each program. If this is the case in your organization, then you may want to take a periodic look at each service; you may be shocked at the drain on your budget represented by one or two programs, or pleasantly surprised to discover that a program provides great benefit at low cost.

• How well are we doing with this service? Since nonprofit organizations are not in business simply to generate large cash reserves, you may want to do a qualitative analysis as well as the quantitative analyses mentioned above. Determine whether you are carrying out the activities of the service well and effectively in terms of your goals and the needs of your target population(s). Talk about how you might be doing it better. Evaluate whether other, better ways exist of delivering the same or similar services.

The questions that will form the basis of this analysis will vary from organization to organization, depending on your needs, history, and goals for the future. Such a diagnostic check can be a valuable first step toward examining the health and well-being of various parts of your organization. Such scrutiny can produce valuable answers or additional questions—either way, it is a helpful step on your way to the development of a sound organizational strategy.

Taking a look at criteria you have developed for new ventures might also prove instructional in evaluating your existing services. If there is a significant mismatch between your criteria and your services, you will need to explore this further. Is the mismatch on major points or less significant ones? Does your service have other qualities that help compensate for less desirable points? Here, again, the art of interpreting data is called into play. If a close match does not spring forth in your comparison, then you may need to decide, based on other available evidence, whether you have a problem, or your existing services contribute to a favorable diversity in your programs.

Armed with solid preliminary data on your programs, you can set forth on a mission to do some scrutinizing with an eye toward improvement. We can all use a little overhaul from time to time. Even successful programs can benefit from some occasional minor modifications. Think about the changes you might see in an elementary school child's handwriting from year to year. In most cases our skills and knowledge mature year by year. Our experience and education in the school of hard knocks may have exposed us to new ways of thinking or new developments which can be added to the way we operate. By critically examining what we take for granted, we can begin to move a step closer to excellence.

In case it sounds like a terrible exercise in drudgery to sit down and completely analyze every detail of every detail, rest assured that there exists a happy medium between ignoring the truth and dissecting it to an excessive extent. You may not want or need to subject each program to careful scrutiny that often; however, allowing your organization to drift into the future without exploring the possibility of change or improvement is also unwise.

VERTICAL INTEGRATION AND THE DEVELOPMENT OF RELATED SERVICES

Vertical integration is an impressive-sounding piece of jargon within the planning field that can also yield impressive results for some organizations. The basic concept is simple. Think of a package of breakfast cereal, and the steps and companies involved in its production. First, there is the supplier of seed who starts the entire process. The farmer grows the grain or corn, which is milled into usable form. This is then purchased by a cereal manufacturer, who turns the raw material into the edible product. Boxes must be manufactured, advertising provided, and the product must be sold and shipped to the grocery store, where we as consumers buy the cereal and serve it each morning without a thought of where it came from.

Vertical integration involves expanding your business into the areas that come before (backward vertical integration) or after (forward vertical integration) your present service in this chain of events. More precisely:

• Backward vertical integration is moving your organization back one step toward the product's origin. In this strategy, you expand the definition of your business in a direction that is related to your present business and take over functions that are now being carried out by another provider or manufacturer.

• Forward vertical integration involves broadening the scope of your organization in a way that moves you closer to the end consumer of the service or a step further in the service chain. You again remain in a related business, but assume the function of another organization that may be currently serving your customers after your service is completed or providing the next step in distributing your product.

If you stop for a moment and think, you will probably find that your organization is an element in a larger chain of services or products. You are probably also familiar with the other links in the chain to some extent. In many cases, these neighboring links can be good targets for expansion of the scope of your business. You already know something about them, you are in a related business, and you can assess the prospects of these businesses as potential elements of your organization. Some organizations might be able to look at elements of vertical integration as follows:

• A corporation providing in-patient rehabilitation services for drug addicts and alcoholics might consider detoxification services, the backward integration step that often comes before rehabilitation, or out-patient counseling services, the forward integration step that often follows discharge from a rehabilitation facility. Here, rather than depending on outside providers, the corporation becomes a multi-service provider itself, offering "one-stop shopping" for alcoholism and drug addiction services.

• A hospital providing traditional in-patient services looks at providing out-patient and pharmacy services to the community at large, and leasing space to physicians in order to build strong relationships. In this case, these services might serve the functions involved in both backward and forward vertical integration. Out-patient services, for example, might serve as both the step before and the step after hospitalization for many patients.

These examples serve to highlight how it is possible to expand into "neighboring," related businesses that can provide an important link between your services. They can also take advantage of your organization's favorable reputation to expand your market. If your organization has a long-standing service in a specific area and is well known for providing high-quality service, this can provide you with a strong point of entry into a new but related area of the market. By taking advantage of that reputation, your job in marketing and promoting your new service will be greatly simplified. You may be able to market the service to additional segments of the market, or expand the scope of the services you offer to your present customers or clientele. By moving your service one link down the chain in either direction, you can take advantage of the visibility, skills, and market you have already established. While this concept is hardly revolutionary, it may help you to think of areas that might prove to be ready targets for expansion.

A real advantage to expanding into related areas is that you can become a feeder system for your own services. In the examples above, the detoxification unit can refer to the rehabilitation program, which can in turn serve clients in an out-patient capacity. Or, for some clients, the out-patient system or rehabilitation program may be the point of entry into the system. In any case, the client can be served well within a single system, which results in continuity of care in health care and social service organizations, and a minimization of inconvenience for consumers in other nonprofit businesses. We all like doing business with companies we know and trust. The supermarket is a good example of a business which over the years has diversified into related areas so that the consumer no longer needs to visit one store for bread, another for meat, and a third for dairy products. By developing a more comprehensive system of related services, you offer your clients the convenience of dealing with a trusted friend, and you will also start to practice good business.

PLANNING A NEW SERVICE

If you have decided that you need to expand your organization's scope by offering a new program or service, there are many things to consider. Any new service carries with it considerable risk—of failure, of chaos during its implementation, of draining resources from other programs. In order to minimize risks and maximize the chances of rewards, you will need to spend some time thinking through real and potential problems, and try to anticipate the needs of the new program.

In some ways, adding a new service to an organization is like bringing a new baby into the family. Although the service may be very much wanted and loved, it is difficult to anticipate exactly its needs and personality, its demands on the family, and the sibling rivalry it will create with existing parts of the family. In a shaky, poorly functioning family system, the needs of a new infant can throw the entire family into chaos, and the family can cease to function in a healthy manner. However, in a functional, intact family a new infant can add to the love and happiness of all involved, although the feedings at 2 a.m. and diaper changes are less than pleasant. An organization adding a new service should similarly be prepared for a demanding infancy and a disruption of the status quo; however, if the timing is right, the new service can fit in and become a welcome member of the family.

Analysis of Pros and Cons

Before making a final decision to add a new component to an existing organization, you will want to carefully examine the advantages and drawbacks of doing so. This activity might lend itself to brainstorming with your staff, or privately writing out your own list. Quite simply, you can start with a sheet of paper or blackboard headed "Pros" on one half and "Cons" on the other. Getting a number of staff members with different backgrounds and perspectives to work on this project can prove advantageous in examining the entire picture objectively. List all the reasons why the service is and is not a good idea. Include any possible factors that might come into play in your analysis. If you have been doing some work on analyzing various components of your organization, the competitive picture, and your marketing realities, some of this information might be useful fodder for the analysis of pros and cons.

Let's use as an example a four-year college with a solid reputation in the humanities and social sciences which is considering expanding into the area of evening noncredit courses for adults. The pro versus con analysis might include elements such as the following:

Pros	Cons
1. No other school within ten miles offers a similar program.	1. This area is not prosperous and many adults may not have money for noncredit courses.
2. We have a good local reputation that should ease our entry into this market.	2. Many of our faculty are opposed to this idea.
3. Such courses have been revenue-producing for other schools.	3. Our location is not ideal and we may need to rent additional space.
4. Satisfied adult students may encourage their children to enroll in our four-year degree program.	4. Our staff and faculty are already spread thin; starting and promoting a project like this may be too much to handle.

This partial picture gives you an idea of how the analysis might proceed. As with the SWOT analysis, a factor can be a strength and a weakness at the same time, depending on your perspective and the peculiarities of the program. Based on the above, can we determine whether our mythical college should enter this new market? The answer is no; this decision can be made only by those who can see the college's "big picture." We need to know more about such factors as the college's existing programs, market position, budget, and past track record. These pros and cons, like all bits and pieces of data, make sense only when considered along with other available information. Each will also carry its own weight based on its importance to the organization. Lack of space might be a minor consideration if rental properties are available and reasonable or local schools can be utilized free or at low cost in the evening. However, this factor might be a major drawback to an organization that lacks the ability or resources to acquire the needed space in an acceptable area. Simply counting the number of pros and cons is not a helpful approach to making decisions based on this type of analysis. Suppose we have a list of twenty sterling pros that sing the praises of the new service and only one con. The con, however, is that the service will cost $1 million in startup funds for an organization whose annual budget is a total of $1.5 million and for whom a good year brings $20,000 in contributions. Here, the quality and not the quantity of the reasons given will make the most difference in your final decision.

Organizational Investment

Starting any new project, whether it is writing a book, learning to drive a car, or starting a new service, requires a significant investment of time, energy, and money. This investment occurs on both a practical and an emotional level; in order to bother with a major new undertaking, you must want it badly enough to nurture it from the initial concept to the reality of day-to-day operations. Although we will discuss below some specific costs, such as staffing and budgeting, the issue of organizational investment warrants some exploration.

Certainly more than one organization has dived enthusiastically into a new project only to have it fizzle due to a lack of interest or investment. No matter how good the idea may seem in the beginning, it is important to have or generate enough investment on the part of key personnel to keep the momentum going. There may be times when it is easier to ignore long-term prospects in favor of more immediate projects, but if your organization is to achieve strategic and long-range goals, you will need to invest as much energy as necessary into new projects as well as into the maintenance of the organization's daily operations. Often one person will provide the spark for a new idea, and can push it along to completion. However, it may be to your benefit to attempt to spread some of that enthusiasm around so that the project does not depend on the whims and perceptions of only one person. In any case, the idea must be seen as worthy of investment, knowing that the investment will need to be sustained over some period of time with no immediate payoff.

Startup Costs

If your preliminary analysis is favorable, early in the game you will want to proceed with an analysis of the financial picture of your new service. Like a new baby who unfortunately does not come equipped with crib, bottles, clothing, and toys, the new service will require a significant up-front expenditure in most cases. "Startup costs" is a phrase that can make a program administrator's blood run cold. An estimate of startup costs is not always easy, as it is almost guaranteed that something will be forgotten and nearly everything will be more expensive than you had hoped. However, you will need to sit down with paper and pencil in hand and begin listing all the costs that will be associated with the new service. Don't forget salaries, rent, furnishings, office supplies, telephones, wastebaskets, and brochures. A lot of these items will be one-time expenditures, and the initial pain will be the worst. However, other categories of expenditures will be recurring and will require a significant commitment of resources at the same time that the lump-sum expenses are occurring. Be realistic in your estimates. Unless you plan to shop for office furnishings at your local thrift shop, look at some catalogs and try to get a realistic sense of the costs involved. Ballpark estimates can sometimes get you into trouble if your estimates are consistently low and the bills come in high. A little research at this stage can save some nasty shocks later in the game.

Space Needs

Nearly every new service or program needs a home of its own. Whether it can survive in a desk or requires a new building, most new ventures will require additional space. If you are fortunate enough to have the space on the premises, you are ahead of the game, and can simply move in and start operating. However, some new services are designed to appeal to a different market segment and therefore will need a separate headquarters in a new area, and some will simply consume more space than is available in the current facility.

As your planning proceeds, it will be necessary to give some serious thought to the amount and type of space that will be needed.

- Is office space, storage space, or program space needed?
- What type of location will be best for your program?
- How much parking space will be required?
- What is the approximate square footage of your program's needs?
- What kind of image are you working to convey?
- Have you included ample waiting areas, clerical areas, restrooms, and other spaces easily overlooked in the planning stages?

As you plan the functions of your new service component, keep in mind the amount and type of space that will be needed. While you may need to compromise from the ideal to the practical when the cost estimates arrive, be certain that you will have what you need to run your program efficiently and effectively.

Budgeting

Calculating ongoing costs is a similarly important step in planning for a new service. Estimate how much the new service is going to cost you over the first year or several years of operation. Again, take into consideration all the personnel, supplies, equipment, or other costs you will incur in your new undertaking. Making an itemized list of these costs will take some thought and foresight on your part, and trying to project costs is difficult and often imprecise. Allow for salary increases, price increases, and the ravages of inflation in arriving at your estimated operating costs. This will eventually form the basis of your program's budget. While it is clearly impossible to predict the future, the development of a good estimate of operating costs at this point will save you from unpleasant surprises later when you have committed yourself to a program that may be grossly over budget. Take a close look at the functions to be performed by the service, and estimate as accurately as possible based on your experience and the track records of those with similar services. Be prepared to develop an estimate of operating costs that will become the program budget, within which you can expect to live over the first year or two of operation.

Calculating Your Break-Even Point

When you have developed an estimate of the costs involved in your new service, it is important to take a look at the break-even point based on preliminary figures. Unless you are in a position to take a large, recurring loss, you will want to be certain that your program at least breaks even. Therefore, it is important to calculate how much revenue the program must generate in order to support itself. Even if you assume that you will subsidize the program initially, you will want to be confident you are not setting up a likely candidate for failure that will consume more than it is capable of giving back.

Your estimates of the costs involved in running the program will show a target amount of revenue you must produce merely to offset the expenses and break even. You will need to calculate what volume of business will be necessary in order to generate that amount of revenue. For example, if your program will cost $100,000 per year to run, then you will need to bring in at least $100,000 per year in revenue to break even. This figure can then be broken down into meaningful units such as number of clients or patrons served, or volume or number of sales needed to reach your revenue target. Once some figures have been developed, you will need to take your best shot at predicting the demand for your service, and determine whether it is reasonable to expect that you can generate revenue sufficient to reach your break-even point.

Naturally, there will be seasonal peaks and valleys in demand and other cycles to take into account, but doing this type of analysis gives you an idea of the level of utilization necessary to at least break even on your new venture in the long run. Naturally, each nonprofit business faces different realities in terms of the types of costs involved and the amount of control that can be exercised over those costs. Perhaps you can scale back costs if your original estimates seem excessive, or phase in your new service in some way.

Subsidizing a New Service

Many new services will experience a slow start in their life cycles. For these programs to be given an opportunity to grow to maturity, it may be necessary for some subsidy to be given to the fledgling until it can reach the break-even point and become self-supporting. Unless you are entering a new market on a small scale, or a large pent-up demand exists for the service you are proposing, you may experience a period of weeks, months, or longer when the new program is not pulling its own weight. Therefore, you should give some consideration to the issue of subsidizing your new service in some way.

Whether by grant money, organizational operating funds, or donations from outsiders, you will need to take a careful look at what type of allocation might be necessary to nurture a new program to self-sufficiency. Look at your cost and revenue projections, and estimate to the degree possible the anticipated market for the new service. Then figure how much subsidy will be needed and from what pool of money it can be drawn. Obviously, if your organization has no excess revenue over expenses, you will need to seek funding elsewhere to start and subsidize a new service. If your financial picture is tight, you may need to specify a ceiling on the subsidy you can provide during the early stages of a program's growth. Lack of operating capital can certainly wreak havoc on an organization's entrepreneurial intentions, and can seriously curtail plans for expansion. Realistically, a small and struggling program must recognize its limitations and inability to take major risks with scarce resources.

Slow Starts and Pilot Projects

For some organizations, a pilot or phased-in project may make a great deal of sense, given limited resources and uncertain market conditions. After you have calculated some of the above figures, you may be scrambling for a less costly way to begin your new project, and in many cases this may be available to you.

Chances are you have designed your service along the lines of the "ideal"; you have envisioned what it will be like when thriving and fully operational. However, for many organizations it may be a wise move to identify stages or phases in the startup of a new service, specifying some guidelines for moving from one stage to the next. For example, if you plan to start a new out-patient service for smoking cessation, which you envision as a large component of your program in the future, you need not hire a full staff and lease a large building to accommodate the few clients that may trickle in initially. By starting small with a few staff members and a corner of your existing facility, you may be able to get an idea of the demand for the service, and generate some initial revenue to invest in the expansion of the program to the size you had originally envisioned.

Naturally, there is a danger in starting too small. If your commitment to a new program is inadequate, you may never get a true picture of what the service might have become had it been properly fed and nurtured in its infancy. Devoting too few resources to a new program is as problematic as overspending, and it will be a task of your planning group to determine a happy medium between the two extremes. Encourage your staff to approach new projects flexibly, however, and be prepared to scale down grandiose ideas to manageable levels, at least in the initial stages. Planning for the small start and gradual growth of a new service can make a great deal of sense for organizations that lack the resources to invest in full-scale, costly projects.

Funding

A central point to any new service is the availability of funding to pay for the services provided. Depending on the type and nature of your organization, you may be supported by donations, grants, fees for service rendered, or a combination of these and other sources of support. Before your plans proceed too far, you will need to undertake thorough research into the availability of funding for the service you are proposing to provide. Assuming that funding will be available for a good idea can be dangerous; you may need to go, proposal in hand, to find out the exact situation you are facing. If you depend on insurance or other outside funding sources for operating expenses, be certain that the program you propose is a covered benefit. If fees are to be collected out of pocket, some sound information on the market for your service will help you to determine whether sufficient customers exist to pay for your services. When you have determined the amount of funding your program will need in order to survive, be certain that it is available.

You will also need to investigate the possibility of competing with yourself for funding. Where will the money for the new program come from? If it originates in the same pot from which your other revenues are generated, be certain that you will not jeopardize your other programs, that is, that you can afford it. If your new program competes with existing programs for grant money, for example, it is possible that you could get both programs funded, but at a lower level. You may also be subsidizing a new program out of operating revenue that could be earmarked for other uses that might benefit the organization as much or more than the proposed new service. In any case, be certain that you will not be negatively affecting your present operations by adding a newcomer.

Regulations

Many nonprofit businesses are subject to regulations of various types from a variety of sources. In some cases, meeting these regulations can be quite costly and can figure significantly into the organization's decision as to whether a new program is feasible. Be certain to check out as carefully as possible how the new service might be regulated and by whom. Investigate licenses, accreditations, or approvals that will be required in order to start and maintain your service. Find out what is involved in gaining approval by these regulatory bodies and remaining an approved service provider. Be sure to include the costs involved in your operating budget. In some cases, these can involve application fees, fees for inspection or survey, and the ongoing costs inherent in maintaining the mandated standards. Health-care facilities, for example, are subject to much regulation, and maintaining these regulations can be quite costly. Don't just take for granted the costs involved or the requirements that must be met. Allow sufficient time and money in your budget to meet the standards imposed on you from outside bodies.

Staffing

In many nonprofit organizations, staffing can be among the primary costs in starting a new service. Whether you are phasing in a new service or just starting out, the number and type of staff needed must be carefully considered. While a program can waste money if too heavily staffed to meet a limited demand, staffing must be at an adequate level to support the needs of the service. Staffing considerations can take several forms:

• New staff who will be needed to support the functions of the new service or program. This is assuming that staff will be hired or transferred full-time into your new component. These staff members will "belong" exclusively to the new program.
• Part-time staff who might assume "hybrid" or combined positions, at least initially. These individuals might continue with some of the functions of their old jobs within the organization, while assuming additional duties in the new service. It is important with such positions to carefully consider the compatibility of the two "jobs" and consider whether the staffer is allowed sufficient time to adequately perform functions in both positions.
• Existing organization staff for whom some portion of time must be devoted or allocated to the new program. Your accounting office, administrative staff, marketing personnel, clerical staff, and others may need to assume additional duties in order to provide adequate support to the functions of the new program. Take a look at the costs that could be allocated to the new service, and make certain that the individuals involved have adequate time to devote to a new

undertaking. Examine the implication of reallocating some of these individuals' time in terms of their abilities to do their existing jobs, and determine whether additional personnel will need to be added in their departments. All of these could add to the cost and have significant implications for the overall position of your organization. Watch out for actions that might jeopardize the effectiveness of both the new service and the old from which the personnel will be "borrowed."

In order to have a chance at success, your new service must be adequately staffed but not overstaffed. You will need to commit sufficient resources to the project to ensure that it receives the attention and care it deserves, but overstaffing can significantly raise operating costs and detract from your service's ability to break even or become profitable.

Transferring existing staff to a new project can often work out well on both parts. An opportunity for growth and change can be offered to a staff member who is ready for a new challenge, and the organization can benefit from the commitment and knowledge of an established employee who is dedicated to the corporation in general. However, be certain that the transferees have the skills and expertise needed for the new venture. An exemplary employee in one position may be mediocre or poor in another if skills, training, and personal style are incompatible with the needs of the new position. If your new project represents a significant departure from the programs you now operate, you may want to bring in outside expertise and new blood. In either case, a committed, enthusiastic staff can make the difference between success and failure in your new undertaking.

Authority and Responsibility

As in any major new project, someone will need to bear primary responsibility for your new service from the development of the concepts to the opening of the doors. Nothing is worse than a Keystone Cops approach to planning, wherein a number of staffers run madly about, and no one is in charge or actually producing anything. It is important to appoint a project manager early in the process who will oversee the service and make sure that the planning is proceeding smoothly. Although this person may not personally be in charge of each detail, the manager will need to do or delegate each aspect of the planning and track each item to its successful completion.

As you become more serious about actually undertaking a new venture, you will need to make a comprehensive checklist of the details to be arranged for the opening of the service. These can range from very minor plans to a full-time job for several employees if a new building or major new undertaking is involved. It can be a sinking feeling to realize that the long-awaited grand opening must be delayed because the furniture was not ordered in time or somebody forgot the phones. Strangely enough, these things can happen. Giving clear messages about authority and responsibility can help you move smoothly through this major event in your organization's life.

Timetables and Deadlines

If you have become serious about the development of a new program, you will need to work to develop realistic, attainable timetables for the implementation of each step of the startup phase. The checklist approach described above can easily be adapted to include time frames for the completion of each item. Work with key staff members to estimate the time needed for each step of the way and develop a timetable that will allow enough leeway for the inevitable glitches. Brainstorm with your staff to gather additional facts and think of details that will warrant your attention as the opening of the new service approaches. The project manager will need to monitor this progress and call a red alert should the project fall behind schedule in any way. It is easy to neglect small details until it is too late. So take care to work from a well-planned timetable.

Whether your organization's primary focus is on new or old services, you will find that your ability to carry forth your mission and achieve your goals depends on a periodic assessment of what you have to offer and how it is packaged. Like any organizational investment, the 1 percent inspiration and 99 percent perspiration rule probably applies. Good ideas and effective implementation can add up to effective corporate strategy.

7

Pulling It All Together

Wisdom is knowing what to do next, skill is knowing how to do it, and virtue is doing it.

David Jordan

If you have put long hours into the development of analyses, ideas, strategies, and plans, you will probably wonder what to do with all of these scattered thoughts and how to assemble them into a meaningful strategic plan for your organization. It is one thing to know what you should do and even how it might be done, and quite another to gear up to actually implement your plans in a meaningful fashion. Coordinating and assembling the work of several individuals, task forces, and committees into a useful organizational plan can pose a challenge.

COMMITTEE REPORTS

If you have broken down your planning efforts into the work of separate groups or committees, one of the tasks of each group will be to develop a report as they conclude their programs. This report should detail the work of the committee, and include its findings, information generated, and its recommendations based on the work it has done to date. Each working group has hopefully produced ideas worth reviewing, and the summary should reflect the work that has taken place. Such reports need not be masterpieces of beautifully flowing prose; a coherent statement of the group's conclusions and recommendations will be adequate for your purposes. The group should also present some supporting data explaining why it has reached the specified conclusions and what the potential advantages of following the recommendations might be. The report should give enough information to be clear on the conclusions at hand, but should not detail every meeting and step of the process. To do so clearly represents information overload, a condition that is to be avoided like the proverbial plague.

It may be helpful to give the committees a suggested format for their report, including:

- *Background.* An explanation of the problem or project and why it has been referred for study at this time.
- *Planning process.* A brief discussion of the committee's work, including visits to other organizations, special research, or other activities that were important to the eventual conclusions.
- *Analysis of the situation.* An overview of the area under consideration, including research findings, the committee's consensus, and a discussion of the pros and cons of the activity or approach under consideration, if applicable.
- *Recommendations and conclusions.* The most important part of the report, this section will detail the committee's recommendations for action based on the work done during the group's life together.

Depending on your organization, the project at hand, and the complexity of the issue, you may want to include other categories as well, or eliminate some of those mentioned above. You will probably find, however, that committing important findings and recommendations to paper is worth the extra bother. Even in a small organization where internal communication may not be a problem, it is to your advantage to have a written record for posterity. It can serve as a guideline for action, and is useful for historical purposes when someone asks three years from now, "Why didn't we act on that new youth program?" Amid the distractions of day-to-day life, institutional memory can be short. Whether or not your organization makes changes based on the recommendations submitted, it is helpful to know why decisions were made and to look back at planning documentation for ideas in the future.

It is also an exercise in good organization to commit ideas to paper and follow them through logically to the end. An idea that sounds great in a brief oral presentation might begin to fall apart under the closer scrutiny of a written report. This type of report forces the writer to explain in some detail how the proposal will work and why, and gives the reader the luxury of reviewing sections of the report that may be problematic, noting points to explore in subsequent discussions.

If you have done a thorough job, you will find that these committee reports are the basis for organizational plans in key areas. The written reports produced by planning task forces can form the cornerstone of your formal plan when the time comes to produce it.

REVIEW AND CLARIFICATION OF DIRECTIONS

When you have formed preliminary opinions and recommendations on areas you have identified as important to your organization's strategic plan, you will probably want to process these thoughts in a more formal manner with key personnel before formally adopting them as your own. If you have a central planning committee composed of top management or other staff, their input on the issues will be vital. The board of directors should also be informed of the committees' recommendations, and their input solicited. All of this will help in several ways your chances of developing a sound strategic plan:

• It will expose your thoughts to close scrutiny by a number of knowledgeable people who may not have been involved with issuing the recommendations. They may have a different perspective, or raise questions that were not addressed the first time around. If your preliminary thoughts stand up to close examination, you can feel added confidence that your original directions have merit. However, if doubts are raised, you have time to return to the drawing board before critical errors are committed.

• Key people who must live with and support the plan will become familiar with it early in the planning process. Even if those present will not be directly affected by planning in a specific area, it is always helpful to have the support of the organization behind you. Their suggestions, as well as their emotional and practical support, can be extremely valuable in the implementation phase.

ORGANIZATIONAL PRIORITIES

As components of the plan are discussed, it will be important to keep in mind organizational priorities and view proposals in this light. In any case, your organization will want to commit the most resources to the areas that best support your overall strategy for success. It is possible that several very sound ideas will emerge that will end up as competitors for limited resources. If it is not possible to do both projects, you may want to use your concept and criteria for organizational priorities as a guide for decision-making.

If you have developed statements of organizational priorities earlier in the process, you may want to test them again at this stage in order to determine whether they will hold up as your planning process nears completion. Your unique set of priorities will form the basis of much of your strategic plan, and it will be to your advantage to be certain that each component of the plan will address and support areas of primary importance to the organization.

It is helpful for any organization to develop clear statements of what is important. Knowing this helps your decision-making process immensely. If you are offered two jobs simultaneously, one involving extensive travel and high pay, while the other is 9 to 5 and offers a lower salary, your decision may be easy if you are a single parent with three young children, an elderly mother, two dogs, and a cat. Even a high salary cannot compensate for your need to be near your home base. Likewise, an organization's needs and priorities can be just as clearly identified if they are thought through carefully.

ARRIVING AT A CONSENSUS

Even if you have clearly stated and agreed on organizational priorities, human beings tend to be imprecise in their thinking, as well as bringing different perspectives to each task. As a result, it is likely that not every-one will see reality in exactly the same light. As we discussed in Chapter 4, it is not absolutely necessary to reach a consensus in the planning process. It is probably more desirable at the stage when you are moving toward the final development of your strategic plan. You should be aware of the need to feel a part of the organization, and to feel heard and understood. We all have a need (however deeply buried) to belong and feel that our existence matters in the overall scheme of things. Therefore, it can be awfully frustrating to watch the entire organization agree to and mobilize for an idea that we find personally abhorrent.

Be aware of several factors in consensus:

- Agreement and enthusiastic endorsement can form the foundation of solid support for an organization and its plans.
- Those in disagreement may need special attention so that their viewpoints are heard and their feelings are considered.
- As plans are implemented, dissenters may need to be observed for any signs of less than wholehearted commitment.

Especially for staff members who feel they are important and should be listened to, it can be quite a shock to see the organization moving in an undesired direction and be unable to stop it. The whole point to strategic planning is assessing the need for change and adopting an organizational approach to the future. It may be easier to survive in an organization with which one does not agree if the areas of disagreement are not spelled out. However, if a position contrary to one's own is formally assumed by the organization, it is difficult to pretend otherwise. This may be a trying time for those who find themselves in the minority or in a less powerful position as a result of strategic planning.

If you do have a great deal of difficulty coming to a consensus on important issues, however, don't be too quick to write the problem off and attribute it to the crankiness of several entrenched staff members. Perhaps there are some areas that should be rethought prior to the development of the plan, and the cranky dissenters are really visionaries. Remember that the world was once thought of as flat by a large number of highly respectable people who had a common assumption. Leave room for suggestions that it may, in fact, be round.

CONTINGENCIES

Since we all face an uncertain future, we may want to openly acknowledge this fact by building some contingencies into the development of our organizational plans. Contingencies involve a multiple-choice reality, and offer the choice of one from column A and two from column B, depending on our needs as the plan becomes reality. It is clearly impossible to allow for every eventuality, and to even attempt such a task invites insanity. One could easily become so bogged down in the development of alternatives that nothing ever materializes.

If you are aware, however, of some factors that may impinge on your ability to carry forth your plans, it might be a good idea to build these factors into your plan. If, for example, legislation is pending that would affect charitable contributions to a program you are proposing to begin in two years, you may need to think of alternatives such as scrapping or modifying the program or developing a different funding base. In such a circumstance, you may need to address the area of contingencies.

A number of factors might warrant contingencies placed on your plans. They might include considerations such as:

- *A change in your financial situation*, including a loss or gain in projected income, a modification of the funding structure, or a change in the ability to raise funds.
- *Changes in the competitive picture.* If a competitor really does open up shop as rumored, your plans will need to be flexible to adapt to the change in the market.
- *The soundness of your original projections.* If your new or existing service does not perform at expected levels, either falling short of or exceeding projections, you may need to modify your approach to suit this, and may benefit from some advance consideration to such eventualities.

If you are fairly confident of your original plans or of your ability to quickly regroup should changes occur, you may not need to develop explicit, detailed contingencies. Think about the need for them, however, and how you will handle changes that occur in midstream. Inevitably, things will not go exactly as planned.

THE WHOLE IS GREATER THAN THE SUM
OF ITS PARTS

One of the principles of Gestalt psychology is that the whole is greater than the sum of its parts. This is obvious if one looks at a human organism as an example. Hopefully, it is clear that we are more than two hands, a heart, lungs, a stomach, a nose, and a collection of other body parts. There is something less definable, called personality, spirit, karma, or essence, which transcends the specific parts and creates a unique, functioning human being. Likewise, to be effective your organization should be greater than the sum of its parts, as should the organizational strategic plan.

If you think about it for a minute, your organization is more than a collection of paper, equipment, property, clients, and staff. It probably has a unifying concept that holds it all together, and is in large part assembled through the dedication and commitment of complex, unique human beings. As a result, your planning activities should strive for an overall concept or unifying strategy that pulls together the pieces of a plan into a meaningful organizational framework.

If this sounds too metaphysical, an example might help to solidify this train of thought. Suppose you are an organization that is dedicated to helping abused and neglected children. Your organization undoubtedly has a number of programs, and perhaps several locations, staff members, and clients whose problems are unique but related. There is, however, more to the organization than any one of the components mentioned above. There is undoubtedly a special quality of parts working together, a synergy that makes your organization effective and in some ways different from other organizations with similar missions. It is this uniqueness that confirms that your organization is greater than the sum of its parts. Staff members may come and go, programs change, and the size, location, and goals of the organization may be revised, but the organization lives on in its own, ever-changing identity. Even threatening changes or the loss of "indispensible" people can be weathered, and the organization moves through what may seem like nine lives.

The strategic plan, as it is developed, might take on some recognizable characteristics of a whole rather than a group of parts. This can be an exciting metamorphosis as a unified direction and strategy emerge, rather than an unrelated collection of programs, goals, and objectives. This element is what makes an organization's strategic plan unique, and helps to define that organization as opposed to others. It will begin to identify who you are, what you propose to become, and how you plan to arrive at your destination. Look for the identity of your strategic plan; search for common threads in your discussions and recommendations, and work toward piecing together the work of many into a framework for the entire organization. Most organizations are prone to occasional identity crises, especially at times of rapid growth or change. Looking at the whole as well as the parts will help the organization to move through the crises toward a better future.

INTEGRATION OF ELEMENTS OF THE PLAN

Unfortunately, not all parts fit together into a meaningful whole. If you put together the carburetor of a '67 Chevy, the carriage of an old manual typewriter, a sewing machine needle, and an English muffin, you have succeeded in creating nothing meaningful with the possible exception of modern art. You will need to be careful that your strategic plan does not contain a meaningless collection of bits and pieces of opposing ideas.

Obviously, the adoption of some plans of action precludes or affects the implementation of others. If you are a small organization and are considering two proposals that pose significant risks and large initial expenditures, you will need to do some work to fit these ideas together into a coherent plan. This might include staggering timetables, cutting costs, or working out some way of scaling down the magnitude of the undertakings. In any case, it will be important to determine that components of your plan can peacefully coexist. If your marketing staff plans extravagant growth at a time when cost-cutting is of the essence, then it will be necessary to find some way to reconcile these seemingly conflicting needs. If you are working toward public visibility at the same time a new program calls for bringing staff in from speaking engagements to work within the program's walls, you may have a problem.

It will be worth your while to work on some timelines and guesstimates of cost in order to be certain that the specific, proposed elements of your plan do in fact fit together. Remember that there is probably no emergency. The world has survived for a number of years without the proposed changes or programs in your organization, and some good ideas will need to be postponed. As we will discuss in Chapter 8, there are always subsequent plans and goals to be explored, and perhaps your misplaced ideas will find a happy home in the future.

DEVELOPMENT OF STRATEGIC STATEMENTS

As you begin processing the work done on your strategic plan, you may find yourself moving back and forth from details to the "big picture." Remember that strategic planning focuses on the "big picture," but that any picture is composed of a number of details that make it what it is. If you can develop an overall strategy and fit some of the big pieces into the puzzle, you may find that the smaller ones are easier to place as you proceed.

In terms of developing a recognizable, overall strategic plan for your organization, you may want to develop a series of strategic statements that summarize for you and the world the direction in which you have chosen to move. In this regard, you need to examine the unifying concepts behind many of your ideas and parts of the plan as described above. You also should work toward identifying major aspects of your overall strategy. Strategic statements might work as follows. You are an organization that has come up with a few major goals and several minor ones for the next three years. They are as follows:

1. Develop an active marketing plan that will allow you to promote your services within a fifty-mile radius of your location.
2. Seek new sources of grant money by creating a development office.
3. Improve the public image of your organization within your community.
4. Work with local agencies to develop a more active referral network.
5. Develop a more active individual donor program.
6. Increase name recognition within the local area.
7. Create a speakers' bureau to increase the visibility of your organization.

You will have developed a set of goals that will be well defined and measurable in your plan. A summary of your organizational strategy based on the above might look like this:

I. We will focus on the development of an active campaign to promote the visibility of our services within the local community of residents and service providers.
II. We will work to improve our funding base through grants and public support so that we can better serve our clients.

In fact, these two strategic statements effectively define the intent of the six more detailed statements. In fact, numbers 1, 3, 4, 6, and 7 could be listed as subpoints under the first strategic statement, and numbers 2 and 5 under the second. In any case, you have moved toward stating your strategy in a nutshell. In order to survive and prosper, your organization's priorities will be public visibility and additional funding, as opposed to an organization that plans to focus on new programs or geographic expansion.

As we have shown above, it is possible to pinpoint your organization's overall strategy in terms of several simple concepts, and avoid burdening the reader with excruciating detail. You also have ferreted out what is important, leaving some of the means to the end as supporting statements. While the detail is what will make achievement of the overall goal possible, it is more important to know what your major goals may be as you move toward the development of the overall plan.

SUPERORDINATE GOALS REVISITED

Perhaps you have already done some thinking about a single statement, or perhaps several statements, that capsulize your organization's overall strategy. In light of the work you are now doing, you may want to reexamine your earlier, hypothesized version of your major organizational goal(s). You need not belabor the point, as we will not do here. However, determining whether the statement of superordinate goals has stood the scrutiny of time will help you to move on your way with increased confidence that you are, in fact, on the right track.

DEVELOPING "THE PLAN" ITSELF

A momentous occasion in the life of an organization is the point at which you feel confident that your ideas and strategies will carry you cheering into a brighter future. Then, you are ready to commit your goals and plans to paper for all posterity.

Writing a document that will summarize a great deal of hard work, details, concepts, and lofty goals is a difficult task. Of paramount importance is presenting the information understandably. Remember that you will want to gear your presentation to your audience—the staff, board of directors, and funders who may come into contact with your plan and will live with it on a daily basis. Plain English works well. Avoiding jargon (unless absolutely inevitable and well defined) and polysyllabic words (such as polysyllabic) will help to make your work readable, understandable, and admirable. Using charts and graphs to present dry data can help, as can eliminating unnecessary detail that can be dug from minutes or early reports if desperately needed in the future.

The Zippy Version

Depending on your needs, you may want to work on developing a zippy, zingy version of your plan for external use and inspiration. You may want to assign this task to your best writer, or seek some editorial assistance. In any case, it may benefit you to be able to present in a brief, readable form the basis of your organization's strategic plan. This might include such important elements as the mission statement, the primary goals, strategic statements, and an overview of new programs or major changes your organization is proposing. Let's face it, only a truly motivated reader will wade through pages and pages of goals, timetables, and assignments of responsibility. For your board of directors, funding sources, most of your staff, and other individuals with a need to know what you are doing, it will be sufficient to know the main points. Being aware that John Smith is responsible for ordering the telephones for the new office two years from next Thursday is not likely to be important to most readers of your plan.

Hopefully you have developed some excitement and enthusiasm for your organization through the planning process, and you will be able to communicate this through your shorter version of the plan. While lying is not in order, this type of document can be a valuable PR tool for touting the exciting possibilities that face your organization. In five or ten pages, work on conveying the essence of the plan you are proposing and the reasons why it is a favorable direction for the future.

The Working Version

In order to track and effectively implement your strategic plan, you will need a detailed, working version of the plan that specifies what is to be done when, and by whom. This part of the plan need not contain prize-winning narratives, but should serve as a guide or roadmap for the implementation of the plan.

In developing this version of the plan, you may want to approach the task as though a group of strangers will be overtaking your organization and implementing the plan solely according to your directions. To the extent possible, indicate what steps and components are to be undertaken in order to move the organization toward the future as defined in the plan. Be as specific as possible in your presentation. Elements left to chance have a good chance of getting lost in the shuffle.

While you will want to summarize the overall directions, philosophy, and goals of the organization, perhaps in slightly abstract terms, you will also want to detail the specifics that have been developed as part of the planning process. Include items such as:

- Some background on the planning process—a brief overview of why it took place, how it unfolded, and who was involved
- A clear statement of your organization's mission
- Strategy statements and superordinate goal(s)
- Specific goals and objectives, both by department and for the organization as a whole
- Time frames for implementation of various components of the plan
- Assignment of responsibility for tasks related to the plan
- Evaluation mechanisms for determining the progress of the plan

These items, as you can see, involve both the conceptual part of strategic planning and the nuts and bolts details of how to proceed.

Hopefully, this operationalized version of your strategic plan will form the basis of your goals and organizational planning for the time span designated. Therefore, it is important to be able to track each element of the plan and be certain that it is implemented as smoothly as reality permits.

Finalizing and Evaluating Plans

We all know about the best-laid plans, and ours are no exception. In order to avoid going astray, be sure that you know what you're talking about when you say, "increase market share" or "improve assistance to the indigent." Without specificity at this stage, it will be difficult to evaluate whether you have in fact accomplished what you set out to do. In this regard, be certain that you have defined evaluation mechanisms to the extent possible. While some activities will be self-evident, such as starting a new program, others, such as increasing public visibility or improving public image, are fuzzy. It would be easy to claim that the goal has been met if one newspaper story appeared casting your organization in a favorable light. However, if you intended the goal to be the development of an organized public relations program to increase name recognition by 10 percent in "man on the street" surveys, say so clearly in your plan. Especially if your organization is large or complex, or if you have a high turnover, it will not pay to rely on memory to move you toward the implementation of your plans. Instead, be certain that you have stated your goals clearly, and have specified how you will know when they are met.

Summarizing

You may find it helpful to develop planning forms, such as the one that appears as Figure 7.1. The reason such forms may be useful is to force some uniformity in the way the plan is presented in each section, and to be sure that key questions regarding actions, responsibility, and time frames are addressed. Perhaps you can adapt these forms for your own use, allowing for other important elements of the plan to be added. This type of summary is useful as you move toward implementation of the plan, as described in Chapter 8. Developing this checklist-type of summary now can help you to work more effectively in monitoring your progress and performance, and can provide a quick-reference checklist for tracking your efforts at implementation. While your plan itself may be quite long and detailed, the summary may serve as a quick guide to the highlights of what should be in progress. You may find that it prevents digging through your entire plan to find whether the new efforts in fund raising were targeted for March or May. In any case, it will pay to develop simple, useful methods of tracking your organization's progress down your chosen path.

GOAL

OBJECTIVE

ACTION STEP	PROPOSED INITIATION DATE	PROPOSED COMPLETION DATE	PERSON TO BE RESPONSIBLE

ADDITIONAL STAFF NEEDED

ESTIMATED COSTS

COMMENTS

Figure 7.1
Long-Range Planning Goals and Objectives

Assembling the Planning Document

You may find that the organizational plan fits best in sections, according to department or function, rather than being integrated in one long, confusing document. You could break the document into sections such as marketing, fund-raising, new services, and changes in existing programs. In any case, be sure that your plan is assembled in a meaningful manner that will make sense to the reader. Some overlap is inevitable and even desirable; we hope that marketing and fund raising will support and relate to new services, for example. But by presenting the plan in sections, you can delineate responsibility and give an overview of the way the plan will work in each department and in the overall organization.

Probably the best way to assemble your strategic plan is in a loose-leaf notebook. This acknowledges the fact that the plan is a living document that will be subject to periodic revision and replacement. One notebook can last a long time when periodically refilled with new, updated information. Using dividers can help in presenting sections of the plan, starting with an overview of the planning process, moving to corporate goals and identity issues, and then to specifics on the future functioning of components of the organization. Although this can produce a great deal of paper, the final product can make the participants feel proud that they have had a hand in producing it. Bearing your organization's logo, the package looks attractive and official. This may seem unimportant, but no one will rejoice in seeing a great deal of work thrown together in a stapled, dog-eared document with pages that come loose and disappear. Good packaging and PR are important within the organization as well!

The Unveiling

The time for corporate hoopla arrives when the plan is completed and made ready for final presentation to staff, the board of directors, and other interested individuals. If you have done an effective job of planning, there should be no surprises at this stage. You should not be casually mentioning the construction of a new building to the board of directors or the phasing out of a major program to staff. You should do the groundwork for any new or surprising elements of the plan prior to the formal presentation so that it is not necessary to stop the presses and run back to the drawing board on major items.

This is the time to brag a little, and let those with a stake in the organization know how wonderful you are and how exciting the organization's future will be. It is important to share the glory; after all, without the support of the clerical staff who typed the plan and the housekeeping staff who emptied the wastebaskets containing the fifth draft of a frustrating report, the development of a strategic plan would not have been possible. Hogging the credit in the top ranks may be construed as bad form. A number of people make the organization what it is, and undoubtedly suggestions and comments from all levels have played a part.

The better part of a board meeting will probably be needed in order to discuss the finished version of the plan in some detail. Providing advance copies of the brief version of the plan will be a good idea, so that participants can prepare questions and comments and be well informed on the issues at hand. The board will play a role in approving and implementing the plan, so that even those members who have not been involved in the process should be knowledgeable about the end product.

The amount of information to be given to the staff will vary from organization to organization. It is unlikely, for example, that support staff will need or want detailed information about the plans for the next five years. Key staff and managers, however, will need to know what is taking place, and may need copies of all or part of the plan.

It's important to gauge by the sensitivity of the information how much should be disclosed and to whom. If you are dealing with issues regarding competitors or proposed changes that are still in question, you may decide against full disclosure of your intentions, even to your entire staff. News does travel fast in organizations, especially small ones, and third cousins twice removed can be in possession of top-secret information regarding your organization. As a result, you will need to walk a fine line between hanging yourself with excessive disclosure and risking the dissemination of rumors and misinformation if too little accurate information is divulged.

The issue of disclosure to outside sources is likewise a judgment call. Those issuing grants, for example, may require some details on your organization's plans and directions. However, you may not want to deliver your plan gift-wrapped to an organization that is competing with you for clients or other resources. An item highlighting your plans in a newsletter or a presentation to a trusted organization with which you work closely can have tremendous PR value if you are aware of what to present and how to present it. Clearly, change can be threatening to all those affected by your organization, stakeholders and staff, competitors and colleagues. A bit of discretion is important in presenting your plan.

CELEBRATION

Hopefully, you do not need a book on strategic planning to tell you that a celebration is in order when a major project is completed. This may be a time for a group gathering at lunchtime or after work, or a simple handshake and private revelry. In any case, you have completed a major task and deserve to be kind to yourself, at least until tomorrow when reality is waiting for you and it's time to implement and plan all over again. But don't think about that now. There's time enough for Chapter 8 when the celebration is over.

8

_____ Living with the Plan

It should come as no shock to you that even the most effective strategic planning will never be perfect. It is tempting, upon completion of your first strategic plan, to sit back and breathe a big sigh of relief because *that's* done. However, the world has an annoying habit of revolving, and you will probably find that something has changed before the ink is dry on your final draft. It would take genius far beyond the human imagination to produce a strategic plan that would flawlessly carry the organization through the next five years. Clearly, the initial efforts at strategic planning represent an important milestone in the life of the organization, but one cannot afford to stop there.

THE RELATIONSHIP BETWEEN PLANNING AND REALITY

There is planning, and then there is reality. Hopefully the two will bear more than a passing resemblance to one another, but you should never ask for more than life is willing to give you. If you set out on a journey and come to a roadblock or detour, you can stop and cry or begin looking for an alternate route. Similarly, you will need to be prepared to deal with quirks and foibles every step of the way.

A key word in implementing any plan is *flexibility*. If you treat your plans as cast in stone, you will be defeating yourself at every turn. Continual scanning of the environment, your organization, and the directions of the plan will be necessary to ensure that what seemed like a brilliant idea during the planning process still holds water.

If your plan needs modification, fine-tuning, and even major revisions as time passes, these are not indications that you have failed. On the contrary, being aware of the need to adjust to reality is a mark of good management. Strategic planning must be based on what is known and knowable at the time the plan is developed. Each day we become aware of additional elements of a changing reality. Although this points out the inevitable imperfection of planning, it is still far better to have an imperfect plan than no plan at all, moving from crisis to crisis and decision to decision.

Planning is never "done." Although it need not consume major portions of each day, it should remain a major responsibility of your management team. While your planning document may look impressive and official and be useful as a shelf ornament or bookend, you will be surprised at how quickly the document can become outdated and obsolete if it is not seen as an ongoing commitment.

If you have been moved to undertake the development of a strategic plan through some external pressure such as the requirements of a funder or accreditor or as a response to a real or perceived crisis, you may find that when the heat diminishes the motivation fades along with it. Again, you can return to business as usual and easily postpone dealing with the future. It may take a real push to sustain a commitment to ongoing planning activities once the original plan is completed. Both implementing the plan and updating it are important activities, without which the original plan will have been an exercise in futility.

IMPLEMENTING THE PLAN

Implementation may be the most difficult part of planning. Often it is less exciting and stimulating and requires a great deal more drudgery than developing the plan itself. The road to hell may be paved with good intentions, but so are the hallways of many organizations.

To be effective, an organizational plan should be used as a guide for day-to-day decisions and operations as well as lofty long-term goals. It should provide the basis for the short-term planning that many organizations carry out in the form of annual goals and objectives. It should be used to make and evaluate short-term goals and plans that are a part of every organization.

While the strategic plan will not form an iron-clad operating manual, it should be respected and followed to the extent possible. If you have done a good job of defining time frames and areas of responsibility, it should be clear how to proceed with the implementation of the plan. Designated persons should be held responsible for particular areas in the plan. They should be accountable for taking the actions specified in the plan and moving toward organizational goals.

Although exceptions and deviations are inevitable, they should be explained and justified; it should be clear that a course of action was amended due to a lack of funds or the actions of a competitor rather than the whim of a manager. Good management is being able to design and follow a sound organizational plan, as well as the wisdom to know when following the plan may not be the best course of action.

EVALUATING PLANS AND PERFORMANCE

If your strategic plan is worth the paper it's written on, it's worth tracking and evaluating on an ongoing basis. To this end, periodic review meetings will probably be necessary. If your management team meets regularly and your plan is not complex, this could fit as an agenda item for a regularly scheduled meeting. However, many organizations will need to set aside a few hours to a day several times per year to concentrate on evaluating the plan and progressing toward its implementation.

The agenda at review meetings can consist of several items:

• *A "backward" review of the plan,* taking a look at its execution since the last meeting and discussing progress toward its implementation. If you have developed a checklist or timetable of events, this will prove helpful in determining whether the elements of the plan scheduled for the last time period have been carried out, and tracking the results or effects of the plan.

• *A "forward" review of the plan,* discussing the events that are to take place between this review meeting and the next. You may want to consider any anticipated problems and be sure you are clear on what will be involved in implementing the next stages of your plan.

• *An evaluation of the items on your plan.* Are they still valid? Have new developments or better ideas intervened to change your strategy? Do you still believe that your plan represents the best course of action for your organization? Discussing such items is always worthwhile, although second-guessing yourself on each minute detail can be exhausting and frustrating.

• *A discussion of new ideas* or prospects that may warrant further exploration. Planning is not limited to living with the plan you originally developed, but should always be broad enough to include new horizons.

Tracking the organization's progress toward the plan is helpful in several ways. It can give you valuable input on whether you were on target in your original projections, and can serve as a good learning tool for future efforts. It also helps to keep us honest and to fight laziness and complacency. No one likes to go to a meeting and admit that he didn't bother to do his job. Knowing that next month one will be called to report on actions or the lack thereof can be a powerful motivator. While fear of humiliation can be a catalyst for action, the reward of doing a good job also cannot be overlooked. Being able to report significant progress toward stated goals can earn the good performer accolades, on which we all (perhaps even secretly) thrive. Peer pressure can help the planning process along considerably if we know that others are taking their responsibilities seriously.

Monitoring the implementation of the strategic plan is a valuable tool for assessing the skills of individuals as well. It can help us to track and evaluate the performance of individuals within the organization. If Manager A consistently reaches the goals defined in the plan or can justify not doing so, and Manager B has a poor track record in this regard, we can draw some conclusions on their job performance. This information can be channeled into performance evaluations and used when making decisions on promotions and merit pay. Again, this provides an incentive to take planning seriously, while giving the supervisor concrete, measurable standards by which to judge job performance. Rather than depending on overall impressions and public opinion to evaluate an employee, a concrete plan provides specific performance criteria. The plan was either carried out or it was not, and exceptions were or were not justified. While obviously this one aspect of performance will not form the basis of the entire evaluation, the employee's ability to move toward organizational goals will be one important factor.

If you have been careful to build in sound evaluation mechanisms, it should be possible to judge the effectiveness of your plan and the ability of your organization to meet the goals outlined within the plan. For example, if you have defined a "successful marketing effort" as one that increases referrals to a specific program by 10 percent, then it should be relatively simple to gather the data to evaluate your progress toward that goal. While simply determining whether utilization has increased by the target amount will be useful information, you may also need to move beyond that simple fact into a more detailed analysis. For example:

• The 10 percent goal has been reached and exceeded for your cancer information hotline. However, during this time period the president of the United States has had cancer surgery and the issue has reached public prominence. Therefore, the increase may not be due to your marketing efforts, and additional monitoring will be indicated to track the utilization as the issue fades from the public consciousness. While your marketing department may be doing a fine job, this statistic alone may not justify a large bonus or merit raise under these circumstances.

• The 10 percent goal has not been reached for your program for low-income pregnant teens. In the meantime, however, the abortion rate in your area has risen sharply and another agency has opened a similar program across town.

In this case, the staff member responsible for the marketing plan should probably not be drawn and quartered on the spot, and goals and projections will need to be revised based on this new information. Your problem in this case may be larger than your marketing staff, and may require organization-wide adjustments.

As always, a combination of solid data and sound management will be needed to monitor your plan and determine the total picture regarding your progress or lack thereof. Good data on all aspects of your organization is helpful to have available in order to determine your effectiveness in the planning and delivery of your programs. Awareness of a problem before it reaches crisis proportions and knowing what is working well can provide valuable clues in the process of ongoing planning.

THE INEVITABILITY OF MISTAKES

The odds of developing a perfect plan hover between slim and none. Allow yourself the luxury of a few mistakes without excessive self-flagellation, and expect that you will occasionally need to drop back and punt. These are merely signs of the presence of humans within the organization, although thus far the almighty computer has fared no better. If you choose not to plan, you will be free of planning errors. Otherwise, mistakes will be inevitable and should be accepted with whatever grace one can muster.

It is probably rare that one mistake will spell doom and disaster for an organization unless it is the result of incredibly poor judgment or horrendously bad luck. Otherwise, you should still have some room to maneuver and will be able to engage in the age-old activity of cutting your losses. Again, your plan or managerial abilities are not automatically wiped out by one error in judgment or projection. If faced with a clear mistake in your plan, you must evaluate your courses of action:

Your career seminars for professional women have been poorly attended, with only 65 percent of your target for attendance reached one year after the startup of the program. You felt confident that the program would be successful, and hired a staff member and printed brochures at considerable expense for your small organization. At this point, the revenue generated by the program is not sufficient to support expenses, let alone provide a surplus you had hoped for to help subsidize other programs with less-affluent target groups. You look at your options, and find that you have several:

• You can scrap the program and fire the staff. Expenses would be cut instantly, but this is a radical and probably unwise move in the absence of further analysis.

• You can determine to whom the program is appealing. The women who are attending may differ from your original target market in terms of residence, income, or job classification. You may be attempting to sell to the wrong market.

• Look at the program itself. Perhaps it would do better at lunch hour than in the evening, or be more accessible downtown than in its present suburban location. Your topics and speakers may not be grabbing the interest and meeting the needs of the women you intend to serve. Consider a survey of attendees or another group you are not reaching to determine their preferences.

• Reevaluate your marketing strategy. Are you effectively reaching women who may want to take advantage of your services? Look into posters, mailing lists, public service announcements, or media attention. Consider new ways of marketing your program.

• As an alternative to scrapping the entire program, consider scaling down, at least on a temporary basis. Perhaps some costs could be cut, or several groups combined in the short run in order to allow the program additional time to find an audience.

• Reevaluate your intention in starting the program. If you had hoped for additional public visibility, perhaps there is a better alternative. If additional revenue was your goal, investigate other revenue producers. It's always possible that there are better ways of serving your organization's needs, and that some serious loss-cutting is in order.

An important part of your ongoing planning efforts will be focused on continual evaluation of the implementation of your plan and the direction of the plan itself. In moments of despair, remember the Edsel. Corporations more sophisticated and high-powered than yours have erred and lived to tell the tale.

THE IMPORTANCE OF ONGOING PLANNING

As we have discussed in the example above, it is never safe to assume that our planning efforts have come to an end. It can be guaranteed that you will not deal with every issue affecting your organization in one planning cycle. To attempt to do so would be to invite insanity and hopeless delay in an impossible sea of detail. Therefore, there are some issues that you will decide to postpone for a subsequent planning effort, and others that will not warrant action at any time in the near future. However, as the picture changes you will find a need to explore previously identified issues or new ones; you will become aware of changes in the world around you and the need to move to keep pace.

One area that your organization cannot afford to ignore is marketing. As we discussed in Chapter 5, the composition of your clients and customers is open to change, as is the nature and character of the world around you. Be especially alert to changes within and without that affect the market for your services. Changes in the demographic picture in your area or a decline in the economy will provide clues to upcoming factors you cannot afford to ignore. A sharp drop in the number of customers from the Northeast or a rise in the number of single parents among your clientele will provide information on ways you might need to improve your operations and reach those in need of your services. Don't let your charts and graphs yellow with age. In all but the most stagnant of areas, this information should be updated at least annually, although you will find it to your advantage to develop reporting systems to track important data on an ongoing basis. In any case, don't fall into the complacency of thinking you know when your assumptions are based on old data. Data can change fast, so that you can easily be operating on outmoded premises.

Your plan should be a living document. A major reason for placing it in a loose-leaf binder is to invite easy updating. If your written plan is more than a year old, chances are that it will seem more like a history lesson than an operating plan. A number of items should have been implemented, and the organization and the world will be a year older. In order to plan effectively, you will need to make a concerted, sustained effort to think about the future and your strategy for facing it.

ONGOING PLANNING ACTIVITIES

If you have developed planning committees or task forces that work well and address issues important to your organization, don't disband them and send them merrily on their way. Your organization will need some sane, sensible structures for ongoing planning in key areas. Going from a formal planning process to hoping old Jim will think to update his plan this year is quite a step down in terms of organizational management. Having a designated group with an ongoing responsibility for planning in a specific area may help ensure that planning continues and is taken seriously.

Planning groups, however, may have life cycles of their own. Changes in organizational structure, staff turnover, shifts in priorities, and changes in the environment can all be factors in a group's eventual obsolescence. You will find that if you view planning as a dynamic, vital management function, planning groups will come and go. Some may be standing and deal with broad areas, and others may be short-term groups formed to deal with a single issue. Your groups may address some combination of short-term, long-range, and strategic issues. The planning responsibility may work best when centralized in an existing body, such as an overall management team that already meets on a regular basis. Whatever structure or combination of structures works for you will be the one you should adopt and support. Sustaining these efforts may be more difficult than initiating them, but in the long run you will benefit from having some recognized structures for ongoing organizational planning.

UPDATING THE PLAN

Although there is no hard and fast rule about updating your plan, you might consider an annual revision of the plan itself with periodic, perhaps quarterly reviews at which detailed minutes are taken for future reference. The new, improved plan that is developed each year may consist in large part of revisions of the old plan, updated to show changes in the internal and external environments and progress toward implementation of stated goals.

Don't overlook new ingredients of your planning process; keep it fresh by seeking new ideas and strategies on a continual basis. An idea that may have been dismissed as absurd last year may have new appeal due to a change in circumstances or the development of a year's additional wisdom in your staff. A new service that may not have been feasible last year due to tight funds may fit in with your improved financial outlook or indications of interest from a major foundation. In any case, be sure to include the new as well as the old in your new, updated plan.

SOME FINAL WORDS

If you have ever studied a shampoo bottle, you may find instructions which most of us fail to follow: "Lather, rinse, repeat." If we did follow these instructions, we would never leave the shower, caught up in a never-ending cycle of lathering, rinsing, and then lathering and rinsing again. Strategic planning is like that. Prepare to plan, implement, evaluate, revise, update, and repeat.

Hopefully you have found some ideas in this book that help you to see, on a practical level, how planning can help your organization and how it can be accomplished by nonprofit organizations of any size. Remember that your organization is going somewhere, and that your efforts in developing a strategic plan can spell the difference between being buffeted by the forces of time and moving down a positive path toward a brighter future.

Bibliography

Andreasen, Alan R. "Nonprofits: Check Your Attention to Customers." *Harvard Business Review* (May-June 1982):105–10, vol. 60, no. 3.

Anthony, William P. "Effective Strategic Planning in Nonprofit Organizations." *The Nonprofit World Report* (July-August 1984):12–16, vol. 2, no. 4.

Cathcart, Jim and Tony Alessandra. "Build the Organization You Would Like to Have." *Nonprofit World Report* (March, April 1984):11–14, vol. 2, no. 2.

Coddington, Dean C. and Jack T. Pottle. "Hospital Diversification Strategies: Lessons from Other Industries." *Healthcare Financial Management* (December 1984):19–24, vol. 14, no. 12.

Espy, Siri N. "Strategic Planning: Guidelines for Success." *The Taft Nonprofit Executive* (August 1985):3, vol. IV, no. 12.

Falkson, Joseph L. and Henry Leavitt. "Strategic Planning for Hospitals: a Business Perspective." *Hospitals*, August 1, 1982, pp. 51–56, vol. 57, no. 15.

Flexner, William A., Eric Berkowitz, and Montague Brown, eds. *Strategic Planning in Health Care Management* (Aspen Systems Corporation, 1981). Rockville, MD

Gruber, Robert E. and Mary Mohr. "Strategic Management for Multiprogram Nonprofit Organizations." *California Management Review* (Spring 1982):15–22, vol. XXIV, no. 3

Kingsley, James F. "Enfranchising *All* Managers to Plan: The Giant First Step to Superformance." *Management Review* (March 1984):8–14, vol. XXIV, no 3.

Linkow, Peter R. "Implementing a Long Range Plan." *Grantsmanship Center News* (January/February 1983):18–27, vol. 11, no. 1.

Luther, John W. "How CEOs Can Help Improve the Odds for Market Success." *Management Review* (July 1984):18–24, vol. 73, no. 7.

McConkey, Dale. "Strategic Planning in Nonprofit Organizations." *Business Quarterly* (Summer 1981). vol. 46, no. 2

Unterman, Israel and Richard Hart Davis. "The Strategy Gap in Not-for-Profits."
    Harvard Business Review (May-June 1982):30–40, vol. 60, no. 3
Webber, James B. and Joseph P. Peters. *Strategic Thinking: New Frontier for Hospital
    Management* (American Hospital Publishing, 1983). Chicago, IL.
Young, David W. "'Nonprofits' Need Surplus Too." *Harvard Business Review*
    (January-February 1982):124–31, vol. 60, no. 1.

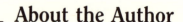 **About the Author**

Siri N. Espy is Director of Quality Assurance and Planning at Gateway Rehabilitation Center in Aliquippa, Pennsylvania. Prior to her career in nonprofit administration, she worked as a psychologist in the areas of mental health and addiction rehabilitation. She has been associated with nonprofit organizations since 1976.

Ms. Espy holds a B.S. in psychology from the University of Pittsburgh and an M.A. in clinical psychology from Miami University, and is currently working toward an M.B.A. at Robert Morris College.